The Small Business Start-Up Guide

A Surefire Blueprint to Successfully Launch Your Own Business

Hal Root and Steve Koenig

Copyright © 1994, 1998, 2002, 2005 by Hal Root and Steve Koenig
Cover and internal design © 2005 by Sourcebooks, Inc.

Published by Sourcebooks, Inc.
P.O. Box 4410, Naperville, Illinois, 60567-4410
(630) 961-3900
Fax: 630-961-2168
www.sourcebooks.com

Originally published in 1994.

The Library of Congress catalogued the previous edition of the book as follows:

Root, Hal.

  The small business start-up guide: a surefire blueprint to successfully launch your own business / by Hal Root & Steve Koenig.—3rd ed.

     p. cm.

  ISBN 1-4022-0004-8 (Paperback)

 1. New business enterprises—United States—Handbooks, manuals, etc.

I. Koenig, Steve. II. Title.

  HD62.5 .R66 2002

  658.1'1—dc21

                                                                    2002009772

Printed and bound in the United States of America
VP 20 19 18 17 16 15 14 13 12 11

Contents

Introduction

The small business is the backbone of the American economy. In a sense, it always has been. From the first shopkeepers of the thirteen colonies to the local restaurateurs of today, small business has been the one constant economic force in America. Today, fully one half of all workers in the private sector are employed by the nation's twenty-two million small businesses.

Corporations, partnerships, and sole proprietors of every size and importance generate half of our country's gross domestic product and pay $1.5 trillion in payroll. Small office/home office (SOHO) businesses are ever-increasing parts of this business mix. The importance of small business is not lost on you because you have made the first crucial decision: to go through the processes of starting a successful one.

Chances are, you are one of the millions of Americans employed by a large company, the government, agriculture, or a nonprofit organization, or you are unemployed and looking for a change. Whatever your reason, you have decided to purchase this book, and by doing so, you have decided to join the small business economic juggernaut. Maybe your business will be part-time and home-based. Maybe you will decide to chuck it all and go full-time, sinking all your time and money into it. Whatever you decide, you have picked our book to help guide you through the start-up, and we will do just that.

The Small Business Start-Up Guide is a fact-filled account of the do's and don'ts of starting a small business in the twenty-first century. The pertinent information is presented without the clutter of gregarious psychological booster material. You can get that somewhere else. However, it is necessary to be serious and excited about your proposed business, which is why we wrote this book in a style that is easy to follow and quick to read. The fluff and repetition common in so many books is omitted, leaving you with, as they say, just the facts, ma'am.

Although intended for a beginner, an established businessperson also can use this as a reference guide, or better yet, give it to another potential entrepreneur to read. The more people who know the basic, commonsense facts about starting a business, the better. The number of home-based businesses has ballooned to over three million. Coupled with the nine to ten million Americans who are employed by a company but work at home, you can see a definite trend.

In this age of highly accessible technology, it might be the best time ever to start a small business. The availability of good business-quality personal computers and software has never been better or cheaper. Fax, modems, powerful computers and software, and the Internet all give small businesses a much more level playing field with the larger companies than ever before. Dot-com mania has died down, and brick-and-mortar businesses coexist with cyber businesses, boosting both in ways no one thought possible. Plus, even the smallest business can generate a big-business look and appearance with technology, software programs, and the Internet. Couple the information and technology booms with low interest rates, current and future federal small business reforms, and tax cuts, and you get the perfect climate in which to start a small business.

We don't want to deny the fact that every business faces immutable problems and challenges that are constant over time. With more people starting small businesses, especially home-based businesses, competition is fierce, but the Small Business Administration reports that at least two-thirds of new businesses are in business for at least two years, and bankruptcies are down from around 70,000 a few years ago to around 35,000 now. Competition may be fierce, but the economy and the success of entrepreneurs proves that this is an excellent time to start a business.

Now a word about this book. It is divided into thirteen chapters with four appendixes and an index. The first twelve chapters deal with the preliminary tasks, research, and preparation needed to start a small business; the pros and cons of various business entities; how to actually start each type of entity; and useful start-up information about vital issues such as insurance, taxes, and financing that can be used at start-up and even while running the company.

Chapter 13 consists of a complete listing of the general requirements of all fifty states and the District of Columbia for starting sole proprietorships, partnerships, limited liability companies, and corporations. Specific resources and services offered in each state are also listed, as are addresses, websites, and phone numbers of state and federal assistance centers.

Four appendices conclude the book. Appendix A lists the Small Business Administration's publications. Appendix B lists various state tax obligations. Appendix C lists some interesting start-up business statistics. Finally, Appendix D contains all of our worksheets for handy photocopying and easy use.

As we will state often, this book should in no way be considered a legal guide. *Never* take legal advice from anyone but a lawyer. However, the information contained herein is factual and researched. Any omissions or errors are purely unintentional. The authors assume no responsibility for misinterpretation, unintentional error, or misprints. This is a guide to use along with the professional and legal help you seek. It is a very informative overview designed to get you thinking about the pitfalls and possibilities ahead. By recognizing the pros and cons of starting a small business, you will be better able to deal with the complexities of running your business later. We say this because in March of 1991, we incorporated as Root & Koenig, Inc. The process was filled with headaches, technicalities, and little problems that got larger. The entire process, from seeing a lawyer to getting the last document we needed, was an incredible two and a half months. Some of this was due to bureaucracy, but most was due to our own ignorance of the proper procedures and requirements.

What we would have given for a straightforward, concise guide to incorporation and starting up a business. We did not need motivation or books describing trends in businesses. We needed solid information without all the accompanying fluff. Unfortunately, all we found at the local bookstores were motivational and trendy books. While the books might have been relevant to some, to us they were simply impediments to finding the information we needed. The solid how-to on starting a business was elusive, so we decided that we would share with you the things we found out firsthand—the hard way.

On the personal side, we would like to thank the staff at Sourcebooks for help and consul. Particular thanks go to Dominique Raccah, the publisher who first gave this book a chance, and to Jennifer Fusco and Peter Lynch.

We hope *The Small Business Start-Up Guide* is useful in the formation of your small business, whatever its size. Wishing you luck, success, and profits!

—Hal Root and Steve Koenig
January 2006

Chapter

Are You Really Ready? Questions to Ask Yourself at Start-Up

▶ **Am I ready for this?**

▶ **Can I handle the responsibilities?**

▶ **Do I have the serious motivation to succeed?**

▶ **Am I prepared to compete?**

▶ **The complete start-up questions**

By purchasing this book, you have decided to join the swelling ranks of small business owners and entrepreneurs. The time for procrastination is over. You have decided that your business idea is feasible and that you will begin the process of actually starting that small business. We think that's great.

But before you actually proceed with the start-up procedures, you should take some time to prepare yourself for what is going to happen. Starting your small business will seem easy compared to what happens next: making that business work. While this book is devoted to starting, rather than running, a small business, we feel now—in the beginning—is the time to ask vital questions about yourself, your goals, and the your business idea in general. Maybe you have already done that; maybe you have asked every imaginable question of yourself and your business. That's good. But chances are you have not asked enough questions. No one can ever question a business idea enough.

You also have to be innovative enough to look ahead. For instance, in 1975 there was no personal computer market, but a handful of innovators and forward-thinking computer enthusiasts believed that people would want a computer in their homes. The result—well, you know the result. Had those people decided there was no market for home PCs, Apple, Microsoft, and scores of firms would not exist. Nothing is disingenuous or wrong about starting a business in uncharted territory or with lingering questions. But by asking questions and then researching the answers—or thinking about them—you can highlight and eliminate many problem areas before you start. Then, while you're running your business, you can tackle the lingering questions.

It is sheer suicide to go into business without being motivated or prepared for the responsibilities. Believe it or not, being motivated does not mean not having doubts. Everyone has doubts, even successful entrepreneurs. It's human nature. Rather, proper motivation means confronting and conquering your doubts before turning to the fulfillment of your dreams. Your motivation has to last before, during, and after you start your business. If you can accomplish this, you will be on your way to success, rather than one of the thousands of businesses failed or bankrupt each year. That is, you must have an underlying desire, need, or want in order to keep the fire of your dream alive, especially during the lean start-up times.

Whatever your motivation—you hate the boss, you have a great product or skill, or you just want to work for yourself—now is the time to solidify it by questioning it.

Am I Ready for This?

The answer to this question will most likely be yes. However, make sure it is an honest yes before beginning your journey. There is nothing wrong with admitting that you are not ready, that starting a business is too much for you to handle at a certain time (one reason people get partners). So if you do not think you are ready, step back, analyze the reasons you believe you're not ready, and take corrective action. Maybe you need some time to distance personal problems from your start-up. Maybe you need to do more research or planning first. If you just don't have the money, try to find a way to get it. Whatever the answer, you will be glad you confronted this question early on. Nothing is worse than external or internal distractions that keep you from devoting time to your business.

Can I Handle the Responsibilities?

Can you handle extreme pressure from your business, yourself, and your family and friends, all of whom will complain that they don't see you enough? You must be prepared for this challenge more than any other because it is personal in nature.

Do I Have the Serious Motivation to Succeed?

Being a modern American small businessperson is not easy. You need staying power to become a businessperson in today's high-pressure, highly competitive small business world. All companies, regardless of size, must change and adapt to the environment and current trends in order to survive and flourish. Staying put does not win the race. Can you, as a small businessperson, change and accept new ideas or methods in order to keep or gain market share?

Initially, you will have a hectic and possibly frustrating time starting your small business. After all, you have to sell your product or service, deliver it to your customers' satisfaction, and maintain the momentum of your start-up. Then comes more twelve- and fourteen-hour work days, seven-day work weeks, and self-sacrifices that must be endured for whatever period of time it takes you to be successful. And once "there"—wherever it is your goals take you—you must continually strive for better and more success. This is what staying power is all about. Those who can change and adapt, and work hard at it, will be successful. Those that can't will work for other people their whole lives.

Alert!

Getting Your Share: With more and more Americans starting small businesses, competition is increasing and market share is decreasing. Your success will depend partly on how you deal with this reality and all other economic and social trends that affect small business.

Am I Prepared to Compete?

Many businesses fail in the first few years for a variety of reasons. The Small Business Administration (SBA) reports that around 550,000 businesses cease operations every year due to varying causes—and about half of those actually were successful at cessation. Nearly 35,000 businesses go bankrupt. Our small business failed because of youth, inexperience, and ignorance. Knowing the odds before beginning a business and then developing a plan to beat those odds is one way to remain competitive.

As we mentioned above, hard work and persistence are important. But so are other things such as timing, initiative, pricing, product, marketing, the economy, and even luck. Those same criteria affect every business in America, though not always in the same ways. Those failed businesses fail for many reasons.

Alert!

Think Ahead: Any set of factors can adversely affect a small business: a failing economy, a poor marketing scheme, a poor product or service, a saturated marketplace, and lack of financing, experience, or desire. Even personal problems such as a divorce or poor health threaten your business' survival.

Since so many people are starting businesses, especially small office/home office (SOHO) businesses, your competition is fierce. While not all are based on your exact business idea, the proliferation of small businesses means continually more parties are going after scarce consumer dollars. You have to compete for those dollars. And against free-trade laws that give foreign companies greater access to American markets. And against small businesses with more start-up capital. And against those well-established small businesses already plying their trade. And against smarter, more informed people. In short, you're up against a lot, but the rewards of success are very sweet, and with all of the help and assistance available to today's small business owner, you're well ahead of your compatriots of twenty or even ten years ago. Ultimately, for you to succeed, you have to take on those hundreds of thousands of other people like you who are starting their own businesses—and beat them. You have to win. Why? Because that's your dream.

The answers to these questions should reveal whether you are ready to really think about your business structure. Even if you have some doubts, and you will, you probably will begin the process of going into business. After all, your small business undoubtedly will be a learning experience, but it need not be traumatic, as long as you plan your course and confront your obstacles. You can't know everything up front, but resolving the important issues will be a great benefit.

The Complete Start-Up Questions

The next set of questions is our Who, What, Where, Why, When, and How section. As you answer these questions, you will begin to see how much or how little you know about your business. If your answers disappoint you, take corrective actions. Research the answers through creative methods and resources. Find out what you need to do if you don't know how to answer a question. Find the solutions before you go any farther.

These questions, as well as your own that you will think up, are good starting points to beginning a business. There is no real order to these questions, and that's purposeful. Just ask and answer them in any order you like. You can think over or skip questions that don't exactly pertain to you.

Who?

1. Who are my potential employees?
   - Do I need any?
   - What skills should I look for in employees?
   - How will I get them and what resources will I use (temp agencies, want ads, etc.)?
   - What is the demographic composition of the local labor force?
2. Who are my potential customers?
   - How can I ensure customers are attracted and stay attracted?
   - How will I get these customers in the first place?
   - Is my customer base general or specific in nature?
3. Who are my competitors?
   - How will I compete with them: price, quality, service, location?
   - Are they too competitive or too entrenched?
   - Are they successful?
   - What are their weaknesses?
   - Is the market oversaturated?
4. Who will be my investors, partner(s), or company officers?
   - Do I need partners?
   - Do I work better alone? Can I work alone?
   - How do I pick a partner?
   - Should I have general or limited partners?

- Will they be committed to the business?
- Will I make the supreme effort to make good use of investors' capital?

What?

1. What is my product or service?
   - Have I sold, made, or offered these products or services in the past?
   - How am I different? How will I differentiate my service or product?
   - Is it different, unique, or better than the competition?
   - How will I pick supply and service vendors?
   - Is there a market for these services or products?
   - How do I fulfill customers' orders or requests? What is my distribution channel?
   - Do I have confidence that what I am making, providing, or selling is of good quality?
2. What compensation do I offer any employees I may have?
   - Do I take a salary?
   - Do I know how to do payroll?
   - How many employees can I afford at different salaries?
   - Can I attract quality employees with the wages I can offer?
   - Can I use non-pay incentives like comp time or stock options?
   - Do I know what competitors are paying employees?
   - Should I combine pay with bonuses?
3. What benefits can I offer?
   - Do I need to offer benefits?
   - What, if any, benefits can I afford?
   - Are there associations or small business co-ops that share group benefits? If so, what are they?
   - Regardless of employees, do I personally need vacation time, health coverage, or a pension?
4. What sources of help are available to me?
   - Can my local or state government offer start-up assistance?
   - What start-up resources does the Small Business Administration offer?
   - What magazines, radio and TV programs, private companies, or national small business organizations are available to me?

Where?

1. Where will I buy or lease an office, store, warehouse, or plant?
   - Can I start with a home office?
   - Can I meet zoning requirements at home?
   - How much space do I need?
   - What office and computer equipment do I need?
   - Can I work at home with no interruptions?
   - Will I need a separate phone line? A post office box? An answering service?
   - Can I afford office space?
2. Where will I get start-up funding?
   - Can I obtain a loan at a bank or credit union? Will the institution loan money for a start-up?
   - Do they lend to SOHO businesses?
   - Am I willing to use my savings and investments?
   - Will family and friends invest with me?
   - Can I get development capital from the Small Business Administration or other state and local government entities?
   - Do I qualify for minority- or women-owned business loans, programs, and/or grants?
   - Should I try to get funding from a venture capitalist or an angel investor?
3. Where do I want to be (in life) in five, ten, fifteen, twenty years? (This is a personal as well as a business question. Answer it and the following questions for yourself and your business.)
   - What are my short-term goals?
   - What are my long-term goals?
   - Are my ultimate goals financial or satisfaction based?
   - How will my business goals adversely affect my family life?
   - Are my goals realistic?
   - How will I evaluate my success?
   - What if I do not achieve my goals—what will I do?

Why?

1. Why should I choose a sole proprietorship, partnership, limited liability company, or corporation? (Also, what are the advantages/disadvantages of each?)

- How big do I need to be to start out?
- What aspects of each entity appeal to me?
- What tax, regulatory, and/or licensing issues will affect my choice of entity?
- Do I need to consider the liability protection offered by a corporation or limited liability company?

2. Why should I go into business in the first place?
   - What are my real reasons and motivations? Are they personal, professional, or other?
   - Are my reasons supportable? Am I doing this for positive rather than negative reasons?
   - Do I want to make a lot of money? Or am I in it for the freedom aspects?

When?

1. When should I start my business?
   - Is the economy—local, regional, state, national—good?
   - Should I work my current job while starting the business?
   - Is my business a growth industry?
   - Do I know when the right time is?
2. When will I find time for family and friends? (We have restated this point for emphasis.)
   - Can I afford the social costs of starting a business?
   - Is it possible to let them work with me in the business?
   - Am I prepared for the loneliness of going it alone?

How?

1. How will I promote my business and/or product/service?
   - What choice of media should I use for advertising?
   - Can I get free publicity?
   - Can I sponsor teams, programs, or events?
   - Should I advertise in the Yellow Pages?
   - Can I use the Internet to my advantage?
   - How can networking at small business organizations and the Chamber of Commerce help me?

2. How much start-up capital will I need?
   • What are my initial fixed costs?
   • What will be my eventual fixed and variable costs?
   • Can I get assistance to determine my start-up needs?
3. How do I manage my business?
   • How is payroll, accounting, human resource management, regulatory paperwork, tax filing, billing, and communication done in the business world? Do I know how to do all of these, especially if I have a SOHO business?
   • Do I know an accountant, lawyer, or SCORE officer who can help me plan for these eventualities?
   • What software can help me?

Hopefully, you have been able to answer many of these questions, and hopefully you have come up with dozens of others specifically related to your situation and business. A worksheet is included in Figure 1.1 on page 12 for you to write questions and answers on. Write down your own impor-

QUICK · Tip

Use the SBA: The Small Business Administration offers a list of frequently asked questions for the potential businessperson; you might want to start there to build your foundation of start-up skills. It's an excellent resource to use in combination with this chapter. It is on the SBA website at www.sbaonline.sba.gov.

tant questions as they come to you; answer them immediately or return to them after you gather more information.

Asking and answering these and future questions is the most vital thing you can do at this stage. If you go into business thinking you have all the answers and don't need to know what the questions were, you will end up a failed business from the start.

As noted, these questions can be asked and answered in order to help shape your initial business plan and influence your start-up operations.

Chapter 3 explores research and start-up planning and contains useful information on how to find answers to many of the questions you ask. You will then use the answers as foundations to the various parts of your business plan, explained in Chapter 4. Here you will learn how all the information you gathered can be integrated into your business plan.

No doubt you might have some lingering questions that seem to defy answers. That's OK. As long as you honestly answer the bulk of your important questions, you will be in a great position to move ahead. You will have answers and rock-solid self-motivation that should be a driving force behind your business start-up. Proper motivation ensures that you will stick to your plans with the discipline necessary in running a small business.

Figure 1.1: **QUESTIONS AND ANSWERS WORKSHEET**

Q._____

_____

A._____

_____

_____

Q._____

_____

A._____

_____

_____

Q._____

_____

A._____

_____

_____

Q._____

_____

A._____

_____

_____

Chapter  2

The Eight Great Steps to Start-Up Success

- ▶ **Determine your product or service**
- ▶ **Research your idea**
- ▶ **Develop a business plan**
- ▶ **Consult a lawyer and an accountant**
- ▶ **Determine your organization type**
- ▶ **Seek government help**
- ▶ **Start your business**
- ▶ **Seek sources of financing**

After you get the itch to start a business, the cycle begins to take on a life of its own. After you decide you have a product or service that will appeal to a segment of the market, and that you have the determination to do it right, you have to begin the process, which includes research, writing a business plan, filing forms, obtaining licenses, and, finally, conducting business. By following the guidance in this book, you can eliminate uncertainty about what steps to take, and this smoothness will allow you to concentrate on running your business after all the requirements of start-up are complete. If your start-up is successful, it will impart that much more confidence as you continue. A bad experience in the beginning can taint your whole operation.

The process of starting a small business, from idea to entity, can be broken down into a series of stages or steps. In this chapter, we have broken down the process into the following eight easy steps that you can use as a guideline. The idea is to follow each step in order, thus staying organized and eliminating possible confusion. Each step pushes the process forward until, by the final step, you are actually in business.

The Eight Great Steps

Although no two start-ups are the same, most will follow an underlying set course. This chapter describes such a course. This eight-step process is generic in nature and meant to cover every type of start-up, from sole proprietors to corporations. Obviously, some of the steps will not have the same bearing on certain entities as they will on some of the others. For instance, a corporation will probably develop a much more extensive business plan than a simple sole proprietorship. Conversely, a sole proprietor may not necessarily need to consult a lawyer or an accountant. The key with this guide is to use it as a flexible, all-purpose list. If one step does not pertain to you, skip it.

Figure 2.1: **THE EIGHT GREAT STEPS**

The eight great steps to launching a successful business are as follows:

1. Determine your product or service

2. Research your idea

3. Develop a business plan

4. Consult a lawyer and an accountant

5. Determine your organization type

6. Seek government help

7. Start your business

8. Seek sources of financing

The eight steps in Figure 2.1 will guide you through the rest of this book. They serve as a further impetus to complete thorough research on your business and the federal and state governments' business requirements. We have included a checklist in Figure 2.4 on page 25 to help you follow the steps in order, to make notes where needed, and to check off each completed step. In Appendix C on page 237 is the Vital Start-Up Information Worksheet, intended to prominently organize all of your vital statistics for your own use. You will use all of this information in a later chapter when you determine what entity to become.

Step one: Determine your product or service

This step is where you will determine what product or service you have decided to offer consumers. Even if you have done it already, now is the time to hone the idea and shape its actual identity.

If your business will be a service, define what exact services you will offer and how. For instance, if you open an accounting firm, you need to define what services you will offer: general services for the whole market or specific services for market niches like tax accounting or business accounting.

If you decide to open a clothing store, you must decide what type of clothing you will sell. You have to decide where you will sell it and how you will obtain the clothes for resale. In short, prepare an organized outline of every part of the service (this is different from the business plan, discussed later). Know what you are going to provide and how you plan on providing it.

QUICK Tip

Describe Your Product: A product prospectus is simply a short report on your product—how it is made, its uses, and how it is better than similar existing products. If it is a unique or new product, you might have to obtain a patent or trademark. See Chapter 12 for the appropriate addresses.

If your business is product-driven, you must do one of two things. Write a product prospectus and make a model of it first so that you and others see what it is you are making, or you might contract a company to make a model. Either way, you must have a physical example of your product and a statement of what it will do.

Time Frame: Product/service generation and research may take weeks, months, or even years, but it is a crucial step. If you are developing a product, make sure you offer the best you can; it may take more time, but it will be financially well worth it.

Step two: Research your idea

You can never have too much information, especially in the competitive world of small business. This vital step is intended to allow you to sharpen your knowledge of business and your chosen field. While you are honing your idea, go to anyone and everyone you can think of for information. This includes the Small Business Administration, the Internal Revenue Service, state and local government entities, trade organizations, small business organizations, and any other resource. You can ask for a list of their publications, and services and products relevant to your small business idea (and for start-ups in general). See Chapter 12 for a variety of useful sources.

Gather this information and begin poring over it in anticipation of writing your business plan. Some of the information might also influence the final shape of your service or product.

Your research is also conducted in accordance with the questions we asked you in the first chapter. These can be used as a basis for general research on all aspects of business. Additionally, ask your own unique questions and provide your own resources for answering them. Chapter 3 explains a variety of research resources and unique ideas. The results of steps one and two will culminate in a business plan.

 **Time Frame:** Researching your idea might take weeks, months, or even years, but it is a vital step that should be given ample personal resources. It may take up to a month to order and receive SBA, IRS, and other publications and information, so do it early in the process. While waiting, you can meet with local resources such as SCORE officers or local businesses and suppliers.

Step three: Develop a business plan

This is a very important step and one you must do regardless of the size of your business. This step should be done after steps one and two, but really can be done concurrently or as you gather the information from your research. It might also overlap into some of the steps that follow.

The importance and scope of your plan depends on several factors, but all businesses should develop one. A detailed business plan outlines your business start-up and the first six months to one year of operation. It will also include projections for three, five, or ten years down the road. This plan is your blueprint to success that in essence will guide your every business decision for the foreseeable future. You will want to be careful and thorough in its preparation.

QUICK Tip

Business Plans Vary: The size, type, and nature of your business will determine the depth and scope of your plan. The SBA, and in particular its SCORE program, may be able to lend technical and practical advice. Contact the SBA office in your area for more information. In addition, private companies provide consulting services to businesses in areas such as marketing, personnel, finance, and so on. For the SOHO business, these services might be expensive, but the cost might be worth it.

The business plan is discussed in more detail in Chapter 4, "Your First Business Plan." Each of the parts of a business plan defines and molds your business concept in one way or another. By thoroughly preparing each section, you will obtain that blueprint, which will also serve as a springboard to obtaining financing. With initiative, hard work, and patience, you will produce a great written business plan to guide your small business each step of the way.

Time Frame: The time needed to develop a business plan depends on the factors mentioned above. For a SOHO business, you might need to spend two weeks to one month on your plan. For larger businesses, a month to several months may be needed. Some people even spend a year writing and rewriting their plans until they are as thorough and professional as possible.

Step four: Consult a lawyer and an accountant

You may need a lawyer and an accountant for consultation on legal and tax issues. They can be of great help in many areas, especially when it comes to dealing with government regulations and small business legal issues. The SOHO may not need any consultations except when issues of zoning or regulations come up. If you intend to form any other entity, you might want to see an accountant for tax consultations and a lawyer for specific legal advice on regulations, state requirements, and licensing information.

Try visiting business lawyers and accountants who handle small businesses. They may have more detailed information for you. Additionally, if you cannot afford either, some communities have a low-cost incubator and quasi-governmental business consulting centers that offer assistance. A list of questions to help you have in-depth and well-informed conversations with a professional lawyer and accountant is included in Figure 2.2

Figure 2.2: QUESTIONS FOR LEGAL AND ACCOUNTING PROFESSIONALS

If you need to consult an accountant or a lawyer, keep in mind these specific questions. These are by no means exhaustive, but will at least get you started in the right direction.

Ask Both

• Is my choice of organization type right, in your opinion?

Ask an Attorney

• What forms need to be filed for certain entity types? Make a list of them and ask him or her to explain the purpose of each.

• What zoning or commerce regulations are there in my chosen field of business?

• Are there any other local restrictions?

• What services can you offer after I start my business? What are your fees?

Ask an Accountant

• What is the tax effect of choosing various entity types?

• What taxes do various entity types need to plan for?

• When do I need to pay them?

• How do I pay them?

• How should I handle accounting?

• When should my accounting year begin and end?

If you have it ready (and you should) take your business plan to the lawyer and accountant if you need to see either. This will give them a better understanding of your business. Part of the reason you may need to see an attorney and/or accountant is to determine which business entity to become. Both can offer practical advice on this issue, which you can use in step five.

Time Frame: After you have completed your business plan, you should go talk to a professional accountant and lawyer. A few days is all that is usually necessary, although you may decide to wait until you are 100 percent ready. If you need a lawyer to handle an incorporation, you will want to get a list of fees and services. You might also have to see an attorney or accountant after step five as well.

Step five: Determine your organization type

The next step is to decide what entity is best for your business. Although some states differ, most will offer the following listed organizational types in order of simplest to most complex: sole proprietor, general partnership, limited partnership, limited liability limited partnerships (some states have these), limited liability company and partnership, and corporation. Corporations can be either C (regular) or S (Subchapter S), profit or non-profit, close corporation, or professional corporations. Generally, you will want to form a for-profit company.

Determining your business entity depends on many factors, including tax liability and rates, legal liability needs, business size, business type, capital (lack or possession of), personal preferences, needs, and/or future business plans. When you sit down to determine your business, think about what you will be doing and what types of business entities best protect your interests with the minimum of government interference and taxation.

Low requirements are demanded of sole proprietorships and partnerships, while limited liability companies and corporations have more requirements and legal obligations. Each type is examined in Chapter 5, where a list of pluses and minuses rates each entity type. Your lawyer and accountant can help you make this decision if you're still unsure.

SOHO businesses are often the simplest business entities because their needs are the simplest. If you start an at-home business, be aware that you may need liability protection or the structure offered by a more complex business entity. Although there are requirement and cost differences between simple and complex entities, you should not sacrifice your business needs for simplicity or cost's sake. A worksheet in Chapter 5 will help you make this decision.

Time Frame: When determining which type of organization your business will be, the goal of thorough research will dictate how long it will take. It may take a day or two or up to a week. This can be done concurrently with the steps above, but you may want to wait to make the final decision after you have consulted the right professionals.

Step six: Seek government help

After researching and writing your business plan, consulting professionals, and solidifying your business entity, you might want to pursue this optional step. Consultation with your local SBA or SCORE office might provide you with further sources of government assistance. A SOHO business might pursue this step in lieu of seeing accountants or lawyers, if only to save money. Additionally, these government organizations can inform you how to obtain loans, start-up assistance, local information, minority and women's business assistance, and practical advice, especially from SCORE officers. Chapter 12 lists the various Small Business Administration programs and services. Appendix A lists SBA publications.

These agencies deal with small and new businesses every day and can provide you with expert and friendly advice. At SCORE, retired executives will try to assist you and answer questions or concerns you might have.

 **Time Frame:** Seek governmental help the same week you see the lawyer and the accountant, or in lieu of either. It might help if you know what entity you will become before seeing them; however, they may also be able to help you make that decision.

Step seven: Start your business

Now that you know what type of business entity you are set to become, the next thing to do is file the necessary forms and pay any filing and/or licensing fees. The listings in the second part of the book give state requirements for each type of entity. Generally, you will do five things in this step, as shown in Figure 2.3.

Figure 2.3: FIVE STEPS TO BUSINESS START-UP

1. File for a Federal Tax ID number (FEIN)
2. Prepare and file any required state forms or licenses
3. Register with your state revenue department
4. Check local requirements/licensing
5. Set up a bank account

If you need a lawyer to assist you, he or she will prepare the forms when you first visit. After a second visit, he or she will ask you for specific information, including company name, officers, and so on. A week or maybe two weeks later, the forms should be ready for you to sign. They will probably be mailed to you: Read them over carefully and do not be afraid to ask the attorney questions. Always make sure either you or your lawyer fills out any necessary state forms such as sales tax ID number forms, withholding forms, and licensing paperwork. In addition, apply for a Federal Employer ID number by filing form SS-4. This number is used to identify you as an employer for purposes of tax reporting.

Your state revenue department will likely register you for withholding, sales and use tax, and other necessary taxes. Most likely, this is done with one or two forms. Local requirements range from city or county business licenses and permits to city or county tax registration. Your local officials will help you through the process. Usually you will contact the county clerk, recorder, or city clerk or revenue office, depending on your city or state. Your local Yellow Pages will include the proper local numbers to call.

The final stage of this step is to get an account at a local bank or credit union. Shop around for value and service. The fees and services will vary from bank to bank and between large and small banks. Use a reputable bank that you feel comfortable with. Your bank will be important to you, so it is important to have a good relationship with it.

Time Frame: The business launch phase may take up to one month for the whole process to be finished. You can speed it along by using expedited services many states offer for an additional fee. A bank account must be obtained after you start the business.

Step eight: Seek sources of financing

This is the final step, because no one except your mother will invest in your business if it is not a legal entity. Once you have become your small business, you can begin the process of obtaining funding. Several sources abound and are fully discussed in Chapter 8. Banks, the SBA, private foundations, so-called angel investors, venture capitalists, stockholders, business associates, other businesses, and friends and family are all possible sources of financing.

Since this step is done after starting your business entity, you will have your business plan and business structure established. You will want to look, act, and be professional in every aspect of this endeavor. This will allow potential investors a look at your plans. Start-up funding is very hard to get though, so you may have to use sources near to you—yourself, friends, family—until you grow enough to be attractive to a bank or investor. Selling stock by direct public offering (DPO; the first offering is often referred to as an "initial public offering," or IPO) is one way a new small business can get funding, and it is growing in popularity. Most states have specific laws and requirements to follow if you do a DPO, and you should consult an attorney before doing so.

In your search for funding, don't forget to stay motivated even when you are rejected (and you will be). The bank that turns you down today may give you a loan after you have proven you can run your business.

 **Time Frame:** The time period for seeking sources of financing varies, as you may or may not get a loan or start-up capital. This depends on you, your plan, and who you see for capital. To speed things along, gather all of your tax and financial documents for the past three years so you don't have to chase these bits of information around while the bank is waiting.

Technically, there is one more step: start operating your business! Get things rolling as soon as you can. The old adage that time is money is true—especially for a small business.

Figure 2.4: **THE EIGHT GREAT STEPS CHECKLIST**

Check off the box as you complete each step.

❑ **Step One:** Determine Your Product or Service
Date Completed:_____

❑ **Step Two:** Research Your Idea
Date Completed:_____

❑ **Step Three:** Develop a Business Plan
Date Completed:_____

❑ **Step Four:** Consult a Lawyer and an Accountant
Date Completed:_____

❑ **Step Five:** Determine Your Organization Type
Date Completed:_____

❑ **Step Six:** Seek Government Help
Date Completed:_____

❑ **Step Seven:** Start Your Business (File all necessary forms)

    ❑ Federal Identification Number Registration Date
    Completed:_____

    ❑ State/Local Business Registration Date
    Completed:_____

    ❑ State Tax Registration Date
    Completed:_____

❑ **Step Eight:** Seek Sources of Financing
Date Completed:_____

Notes:_____

_____

_____

_____

_____

_____

Chapter  3

Beginning the Process

- ▶ **Researching and documenting your start-up needs**
- ▶ **How to gather information**

This chapter begins the process of going into business. After you follow the guidance in this chapter, you will be on your way to the most important step, the business plan. Additionally, you will discover answers to further important questions.

Researching and Documenting Your Start-Up Needs

Researching everything about your chosen business, from regulations to start-up requirements to sources of capital to suppliers, is vital. Much of your research will be predicated on the simple question: What don't I know? In Chapter 1, you answered a battery of questions. Hopefully, you came up with many more of your own. Chances are you do not have the answers to all of the questions. That's OK, because now you can conduct the research for those answers, statistics, and information.

If you are unsure about which business you want to be in, research several, compile a complete list of all the good and bad points of each, and decide which will be more successful. After your specific idea is developed, we recommend taking six steps to thoroughly research your business proposition, as shown in Figure 3.1.

QUICK Tip

Research Everything: Prior to forming your business, you should be prepared to spend several hours in the library, at the bookstore, on the Internet, at the Small Business Administration, SCORE, or other government agencies, on your state's website, at trade shows, conventions, association meetings, the Chamber of Commerce, business development centers, and if possible, in stores, offices, or factories.

Figure 3.1: THE SIX STEPS OF START-UP RESEARCH

1. List your personal goals first

Building on what you did in Chapter 1, conscientiously write down what you want to do with your life. List your likes, dislikes, and goals (for your financial life and your family life). Take a great deal of time with this and be thorough. The more you are willing to admit to yourself, the more you will channel that into your business goals. Be sure to list where you want to be in three, five, and ten years.

2. List your business goals

Write down your short- and long-term goals for your business. Ask yourself the questions from Chapter 1 to help shape and mold those goals. Be sure to include questions you have developed on your own. You may not have answers to all of the questions or you may be unsatisfied with some of the answers, and that will spur you to further research.

3. Compare your goals

Consider the compatibility of the goals in item one with those in item two, and determine which businesses will most be able to satisfy your personal and professional goals. Often, your personal goals will dictate your professional goals.

4. Research extensively

Here you simply use or go to any of the resources listed later in this chapter. The different methodologies of research and fact finding should be fairly all-encompassing. Do not limit yourself to one type of research or one source for your information. Remember, you can never have enough information. Your research will be done to answer your questions, support your business idea, and provide you with complete information for current or future use.

5. Analyze the data and information

After you have gathered your important information in one place, take some time alone or with your business partner(s) to pore over it. Your research should provide answers to soothe your nervousness or apprehensions, and it will provide the framework for your all-important business plan, covered in the next chapter.

continued

6. Re-research

After you have gathered your information, you may discover you need still more facts or answers. Why? Because your research will inevitably raise new questions that need new answers. Don't be alarmed, as this is normal. Any process as involved as starting a business is bound to be complex and time consuming, and you must be flexible enough to work with that complexity. If that means burning the midnight oil pursuing more answers, do it. In the end, you'll be happy you did.

How to Gather Information

Now that you have spent time with Figure 3.1, you probably see that researching can be accomplished in many different ways and with many different resources. Luckily, we live in the information age, where the click of a mouse can bring a wealth of information to your computer screen. Information is at your fingertips waiting to be had. The resources and methods listed below are diverse and, in some cases, unique. This should give you an edge on your small business start-up competitors. Many more specific sources of help are listed in Chapter 12.

- Visit your local library, bookstore, or newsstand, all of which contain further resources that will greatly aid your search. Libraries have business sections and most are computerized, which makes interlibrary searching and loaning easier. A variety of books and magazines on business await you at your bookstore. Some of these publications are listed in Chapter 12.
- Use the Small Business Administration's many agencies and programs. Along with the SBA, other government entities provide business information. In addition, the SBA website's vast online library contains a section with small business success stories.
- Talk to a retired executive at the Service Corps of Retired Executives (SCORE), an organization funded by the SBA. These men and women can be very helpful by using their experience and knowledge to aid your research.
- Use demographic data such as traffic counts, population statistics, crime data, census figures, tax rates, buying trends, and so on to get a sense of how your customer base behaves.

- Conduct market studies and surveys. You can do this yourself, either formally or informally, to get feedback on your product or service. If you have the money, you can hire a firm to do this.
- Spy. That's right, if you want to know about prices at another store or how many customers a competitor has, simply visit the store and walk around, observing it in action.
- Work in your chosen small business before starting one. Nothing beats experience to show you the ropes.
- Attend trade shows, expos, and business fairs. These are excellent sources of information and personal contacts and allow you to scan what competition is out there.
- Network with colleagues, friends, or associates. Everyone knows someone else who can help them with some aspect of their business. Use these friends, associates, and their knowledge to your best advantage. Most will be glad to share advice with you.
- Visit local colleges to see if they have any resources that might help you start a small business. Many campuses are sites of the SBA program's Small Business Development Centers. Colleges may also offer some demographic and economic data.
- Use job interviews and résumés to evaluate the employee pool in your community.
- Follow the local and national news. Keep abreast of trends and fads. Often, your local papers contain a wealth of small business news in your community.
- Talk to members of your local Chamber of Commerce. Again, they will probably be open to helping you along. They were once in your situation.
- Use the Internet to open the door to a Pandora's box of small business and helpful government websites. The beauty of the Internet is that one site often leads to another. It is an excellent source of addresses and information. Use the Yellow Pages online as well. Also, the phone books of large cities have a wealth of phone numbers for companies, services, and products.
- Talk to other entrepreneurs who have started their own businesses for advice, information, and encouragement. Many small business owners will gladly tell you what they went through.
- Write to companies and request information on how they started out.

- Buy competitors' goods to compare to yours, and make notes on how they advertise.
- If you know of any, talk to your competition's former employees. They may give you insight into how the competition operates.
- Brainstorm. That's right—use your own noggin and that of a business partner/investor, friend, or spouse to come up with your own unique answers and information. Personal questions can often be answered very effectively this way.
- Attend continuing education courses, often taught by local universities. These refresher courses may contain information or contacts well worth your time.
- Use private companies or private business, organizations, and associations. Many associations exist exclusively for small businesses, and they are often open to dispensing help and information. Join a few.
- Use trade publications. Most trades and businesses have newspapers, publications, or newsletters, which can be of great assistance.
- Use banks, accountants, and attorneys as sources of information. Talk to a banker experienced in business lending—he or she can provide valuable insight.
- Visit your local government's economic development department for information on finances and available programs.
- Listen to talk radio business programs and watch business shows on TV.
- Join barter exchanges to exchange goods and services via barter. This is akin to networking.
- Use a business consultant. Again, this is expensive, but if you have the money, a consultant might be able to help you start your business on a great footing.
- Purchase programs and software from business and entrepreneurial sources. These range from guides on how to start specific businesses, to business law manuals, to audio programs on motivation.
- Use minority and women's groups resources. Often, minority and women's organizations (especially women's business groups) are eager to help those coming up through the small business ranks like they once did.
- Business think tanks can offer useful information, a few of which are listed in Chapter 12.

• Go to www.sbaonline.sba.gov/starting and search for the great Small Business Startup Kits available for each state.

Be sure to mull over government publications and statistics related not only to your chosen businesses, but also to the economy as a whole. The whole economy does affect you, no matter how small you are. Most popular consumer magazines carry a potpourri of items useful to the investor, corporate-level executive, and even mid-level businessperson. You will not find much about small business on a regular basis, though consumer publications often profile smaller businesses and report on small business trends. These publications also provide you with a pulse on the economy, society, trends in trade and finance, and successful corporate businesspeople. With small businesses proliferating, many are including more information on small businesses (even SOHOs).

If you can satisfactorily answer the motivational questions confronting you and you have done your research, then you are mentally ready to be the boss of your own business. The next step is to become technically ready through your business plan.

Although never easy, millions before you have started their own businesses. Not all succeeded, but not all failed. When armed with research, months of preplanning, a killer business plan, and dedication, the entrepreneur enters the world of business with a decided advantage. It is this advantage early on that may be the difference between success and frustration, which can lead directly to failure. You will put this advantage to good use in the next chapter.

Chapter

Your First Business Plan

- ▶ Creating a winning small business plan
- ▶ Writing your business plan
- ▶ Cover sheet
- ▶ Introduction
- ▶ Mission statement
- ▶ Overview of your business
- ▶ Economic analysis
- ▶ Financial analysis
- ▶ Market analysis
- ▶ Summary
- ▶ Appendix

Before every successful business launch must come a business plan, and after every successful business launch must come further short- and long-term plans. These strategic plans are different from your initial business plan, though the two are related. In college, the keystone class in the business program is often a strategic planning course, and for good reason. Planning is the key to small business success.

It is necessary to plan, chart, and dream about your potential business's future. Without a vision, a business is blindfolded and will go around in circles until it finally collapses. History is littered with blindfolded entities—businesses, people, countries—that had no direction, plan, or long-term goals. Our company, for example, was going to produce mail order material (T-shirts, bumper stickers, posters, and the like), but instead of writing a complete business plan, we felt we only needed a skimpy one, and problem after problem followed. We broke a cardinal rule of managing a business: plan ahead!

Your first business plan will be your blueprint for operations, financing, and growth. It will provide a guide to running and managing your company, as well as marketing your goods or services. The plan is an integral part of your quest for financing and capital, as it forecasts needed start-up and operating capital. As you project into the future, your anticipated growth patterns will be laid out, making goal-setting easier to achieve.

Alert!

Get the Order Right: Experts always tell you to write the introduction, executive summary, and conclusion of your business plan after you've completed all other sections. Saving these sections until you are done will give you the perspective you need to write them well.

Creating a Winning Small Business Plan

Before you write your plan, consider how important it will be to your start-up. Although the size of a plan may vary from a few pages to a few hundred, you need not worry about how big it is, just how thorough it is for your needs. We recommend you spend copious amounts of time refining this plan. After all, you may well present it to potential financial backers who are impressed by your professionalism and thoroughness. Since this is the blueprint for your business, be sure to be realistic. Don't be afraid to spend time brainstorming, researching, and writing the plan. You want the best plan, not the one that took ten minutes to write and looks like it. See Chapter 12 for a list of a few books that offer extensive business plan advice, with sample plans for you to browse.

The following are basic areas you must know in order to prepare your business plan.

The idea

You need a business idea: the more original the idea, the closer you will be to it and the harder you will work at it. Bill Gates and Donald Trump both love what they do and are good at it. That's not an accident—it is motivation and drive based on a passion for their businesses.

The simplest of entities (a small retail store, for example) could mean the world to you, and that will make you work very hard to make it a success. You do not have to be an IBM to be a happy business owner. Being unique and having a unique product can often bring about great success.

Time Frame: The first step after picturing your business is to determine the time frame to start your company. It usually takes three to six weeks for incorporation certificates to be discussed, created, signed, sent to the state, and returned to the incorporator. It takes less time for other forms, but you should not conduct business until you are officially incorporated or documented with the state. So from the time you decide to incorporate until the act is final is a minimum of about four weeks.

QUICK Tip

Learn with Others: Be on the lookout for free and low-cost workshops and classes to teach you the basics of creating a business plan, often given by banks, the SBDC (Small Business Development Center), universities, and business planning firms. This would also be a great networking opportunity.

Choosing a name

You will also need to name your company. Remember, most states maintain that the words "corporation," "incorporated," "Inc." "company," "co," or "limited" must appear in the title of the corporation name. Limited partnerships usually must have "LP" or "Limited Partnership" in the name. This varies from state to state. Also, all business conducted by the company must include that title. For instance, if a person writes you a check, make sure it is made out to the full name of the company. In addition, many states require that the name of the company be somehow identifiable with the owners. Assumed or fictitious names are used for companies, proprietors, or partnerships not wishing to identify the owners in the name of the company the customers deal with. Check your state for details. Some businesses are allowed to "do business as" (DBA) under a different name than their company name.

Define your purpose and goals

A vital step is to conscientiously map out your mission and first-year goals. Your purpose should be clear and concise, yet it may not have to be so clear on the certificate of incorporation. Most companies are perpetual in duration. And remember to ask those very important questions from Chapter 1, including: 1) How much capital will we need? and 2) How much do we have? The answers to these questions will directly affect your company's operations, so answer them beforehand.

List your officers and their duties

For a corporation, you might have a list of officers for the board. Write those names down, along with the duties they will perform within the company.

Most first businesses have a board of directors who are also stockholders and managers of the company.

Your office and agent

You will need an office and an agent, often called a Resident Agent if you go the corporation or limited liability company route. The agent who incorporates for you is often a lawyer, but not necessarily, and his or her address must be on the document. The address of the company is usually an office, although it can be a home if you are zoned business or commercial.

Plan your capital requirements

Financially, you must realize that undercapitalization is a major problem of small businesses. You would do well to carefully think out and plan your capital needs before you create a business. Sources of capital are listed in Chapter 8. That's some advice we learned the hard way.

   If you need $25,000 for your business, don't settle for $2,500 and try and make do. It simply will not work. Wait until you can raise more money, and then try to use the money to leverage for a loan at a bank for the rest of the $25,000. By cutting short your capital infusion into your company, you may also cut short its life.

Determine your start-up equipment needs

Equipment needs will vary, and you should shop around. If anything, that is the golden rule in frugal business management: shop around. Most cities have several sellers of business equipment. Call ahead or get their catalogs and compare prices and quality, and then make the purchase. Another route, and a good one, is to get used equipment. Most cities auction off old municipal equipment from time to time, and that is a great place to pick up everything from desks to computers to filing cabinets. The federal government also auctions off a huge selection of items for sale, often at ridiculously low costs. See Chapter 12 for information on other sources of equipment and supplies.

Location, location, location

Office space can be expensive, so once again, shop around. The beginner to business will most likely have to avoid central business districts and high-rent office parks. However, smaller office parks and those located in suburbs or industrial parks are usually reasonable. Expect to pay from $5 to $20 a square foot in smaller cities like Fort Wayne, Indiana. In larger cities, expect to pay much more, up to $40 or more per square foot of prime office space in a major office building in Manhattan. Get enough space for your current needs and your future mid-term goals.

One possible way to obtain cheaper office space (and some government assistance) is to locate in an urban enterprise zone. While the terms may differ from city to city, the purpose does not. These zones are often located in older, inner-city areas, and their intention is to pump money back into the area in hopes of causing it to develop again. Often, the government will give tax breaks, grants, or other assistance to companies locating and hiring in these areas. It is certainly something to look into. Call your city's mayoral office or economic development office.

In addition, some cities have "incubators," or business development centers. These are usually full-service centers offering your new business receptionists, office space, conference rooms, equipment, and so on without the usual high costs. They are intended to aid new businesses in the initial stages of incorporation. The incubator can be of valuable assistance, especially if you have limited start-up and operating funds. They are often run by local or state governments, many in conjunction with the SBA, which has a large number of small business development centers. Check your city government directory, the SBA's website, or call your local Chamber of Commerce for information.

Writing Your Business Plan

A lot goes into a business plan. The things we discussed above as well as the results of your question-and-answer session, your goals and objectives, and your research will combine to create a winning plan. You will pick and choose those parts of your research and plans that have a bearing on your operations and include them in the plan. Focus on the short term in your plan, but plan for the long term. That is, your plan is a blueprint to your first few years of operation, but it also forecasts future growth. This is done to preserve your sense of both short- and long-term planning and to present potential investors with two things: your short-term operating goals and your long-term vision.

The plan should not be unrealistic, though. Leave your dreams out of it, but by all means include your goals. Just make sure they are obtainable and down to earth. Bankers, venture capitalists, and investors know impossible dreams when they see them and will pass you over if your goals are in the clouds.

A business plan has several parts to it. We listed them below and include brief explanations on the purpose and importance of each section. For further in-depth analysis of a plan, check out one of the resources in Chapter 12.

Figure 4.1: BUSINESS PLAN ESSENTIALS

Business plans are very adaptable to a specific business's situation, but all contain some common elements. Your business plan should include the following sections:

- Cover Sheet
- Introduction
- Mission Statement
- Overview of Your Business
- Economic Analysis
- Financial Analysis
- Market Analysis
- Summary
- Appendix

Now that you've studied Figure 4.1, you are ready to think about what goes into each part of the plan. Remember, your plan will vary depending on your size, goals, and entity type. The key words here are *thoroughness* and *realism*. Be realistic when you write your plan. That is one reason it may take a month or a year to write it.

Alert!

It's Not All Smooth Sailing: A business plan should be optimistic, of course, but never shy away from addressing the risks involved in your business idea. Be upfront and honest, and do not avoid the problem areas.

Cover sheet

The cover sheet simply contains the name of your company, the principals, and the address and phone number. If you have a fax number, website, and an email address, put that information on the cover sheet as well.

Introduction

This section is intended as a brief precursor to the plan that follows; it's the icebreaker, so to speak. State your business's general purpose and maybe an overview of your plan that follows. Keep it short because you will have time to explain everything in detail later.

Mission statement

The mission statement of your plan should be your overall company philosophy and your company direction. It should identify the kind of business you will run and how you will be perceived by the public. Therefore, write a mission statement that reflects what you would like the company to be like if you were a customer. Emphasize the uniqueness of your product, service, methods of doing business, commitment to quality and the customer, and overall integrity.

Mission statements vary depending on the type of business, but all contain something on the values of the company, a description of the goods or services, and a statement of customer service objectives. Often, they will contain information on relevant technologies and/or practices that make the company unique.

Overview of your business

This section will be written largely on the strength of your answers from Chapter 1 and your follow-up research. It is the broad description of your business, broken down into specific parts. Again, thoroughness will apply. You will need to identify your start-up objectives and requirements, office location, personnel needs, and product/service identification and description. List your short-term objectives, defining where you want to be in a year's time and how you plan to get there. List your personnel requirements by planning how many employees you will need and what the skill level must be. You may need employees with skills you do not possess. A strength/weakness evaluation of your own skills will tell you what type of employees you need.

Include your management team in this assessment. One way to do this is to create an organizational chart, listing managers and defining their functions. Pay attention to what strengths are needed in each management position. A SOHO business may have only one employee, and that's fine. Just explain that. Other items include a description of what product or service you are offering, including how it is different or better.

Economic analysis

Report on the health of the local, state, regional, and national economy as it relates in general and in specific to your business and industry. Discuss such things as seasonal economic fluctuations vis-à-vis your company and how the economy will affect you. A discussion of your industry and internal and external effects on it is warranted here. List its growth trends, legal issues, strengths, and weaknesses. Your part in this industry may be affected by the whole industry's health.

Financial analysis

This is where the plan gets very technical. You will need to include all of the following in your plan. This part will help you project revenue and will give you a description of your financial state and future financial goals.

List your capital requirements and your start-up costs. Also, you want to list any sources of financing or capital you now have. A banker will be interested in how much money you have and are getting when he or she looks at a loan application.

Be accurate when estimating your projected sales figures. Stick to conservative figures. Support these projections with evidence and statistics. Also present a detailed cash flow section, listing the biweekly cash flow projections. Again, this will tie into your sales projections. This section may need to be extensive, especially if you want to show a potential investor your cash flow growth over a period of, say, six months to a year. The idea here is to show investors when cash will come into the business and at what rates. It will also give you an idea of your company's progress over the first year.

Another part of this section is the one-year budget. This is your first year's operating budget, including your fixed costs, overhead, salaries, taxes, advertising payments, lease payments, and so on. Variable costs will be incurred after your start-up and may add or decrease your budgeted expenditures. When examining the revenue side of your budget, be conservative.

The next part is your balance sheet showing your net worth on a specific date. You will want to include a beginning balance sheet. List your assets (cash, receivables, prepaid expenses, etc.), liabilities (debts and accounts payable), and equity (stock values).

Be sure to include a break-even analysis that projects your expenses versus revenues in a projection that shows what sales will be needed to break even. You can also estimate profits with this analysis. You and your potential creditors will use this to see the feasibility of your business.

A final statement on your accounting methods and credit policy will round this section out. You may want to consider a professional accountant for thoroughness and professionalism. What kind of credit will you extend to your customers, and what will be your policies on bad debts, collections, and discounts?

Market analysis

This section discusses your market, competition, and methods of pricing, advertising, and selling. You need to discuss your competitors and the local market for your product/service. Discuss trends as well, and be sure to show

how your product or service will be differentiated by price or quality and how you will use your uniqueness to generate sales. Include a complete section on marketing strategies and advertising. Another important part is to describe your distribution channels.

Summary

In this section, wrap up your business plan with a few paragraphs of compelling remarks about your business.

Appendix

Show any supporting documents, charts, or indices you desire here. This is not a necessary part of the plan, but provides you with additional space for whatever additional information clearly backs up your plan.

This is a general overview of a business plan. Now that you have this direction, spend some time with one of the business plan books on the market that is more extensive and includes numerous sample business plans.

As for the plan itself, we recommend that you pause after you finish your initial business plan or proposal. This is a good way to get away from your ideas and come back to look at them objectively. Wait two weeks and do not look at the plan or think about your business. Then reread the plan and get rid of all self-doubts you may still have.

You may decide to rewrite your plan once you have cash-flow and want to secure a loan for future growth. Many banks won't give loans to start-ups, but after a start-up can show a sustained cash flow, they become more receptive. And as you expand and add employees or services and products, be sure to revise your plan to include them.

In fact, you may want to revise your plan periodically or write a new two-to five-year plan. This will include many things, including your growth rates and goals after your first year of operation. Chapter 11 includes an entire section on strategic planning, the follow-up to writing a business plan.

Now that you have your plan, you can finally become your business. The next chapter deals with the many options available to potential businesspersons.

Chapter

The Seven Main Types of Business Structures

- ▶ **Sole proprietorship**
- ▶ **General partnership**
- ▶ **Limited partnership**
- ▶ **Limited liability company**
- ▶ **Limited liability partnership**
- ▶ **Corporation (C-corp)**
- ▶ **Subchapter S-corporation (S-corp)**

The modern small business starter has many options from which to choose a business entity. The entrepreneur may choose from simple forms like sole proprietorships or complex ones like subchapter S-corporations. Each entity is designed for different business needs. Every type of business fits into one of the seven main entity types, as shown in Figure 5.1. Even SOHO businesses are covered by the choices of entity.

Figure 5.1: BUSINESS ENTITY SELECTION LIST

The numerous types of business entities are listed below. Overall, the options include:

- sole proprietorship
- general partnership
- limited partnership
- limited liability company
- limited liability partnership
- corporation (C-Corp)
- subchapter S-corporation (S-Corp)

Other less common types include:

- limited liability limited partnership
- the business trust
- and the close corporation

Additionally, all states have nonprofit corporations and some have other forms of nonprofit entities. Nonprofit is usually for a charitable organization or a similar entity, and not usually in what we classify as a "business" that someone would be interested in starting. For information on these, contact a lawyer.

If your small business start-up involves buying an existing business, we suggest you hire or at least talk to a lawyer in addition to an accountant. The transactions are complicated and you will be glad you consulted them.

Remember, too, that in buying a business, you are buying a living, breathing entity that is already up and running in other locations. This saves you some start-up concerns, but also thrusts you into the business world right away.

In this chapter, we have provided a synopsis overview of each of the for-profit forms of business in order from most simple to most complex. Additionally, we list the strengths and weaknesses of each entity. These guides are generic in nature and intended to give you a general idea of what to expect with each type. Remember that in some states, certain business entities have certain rules or requirements that are unique to your state. To find out about your state, consult Chapter 13 of this book and write to your state for further information.

The IRS defines a small business as a firm with annual gross receipts of $10 million or less, and the SBA also considers companies with fewer than five hundred employees to be small businesses. With this in mind, choose your entity carefully to take advantage of tax, regulatory, legal, time, and finance considerations. Do not become the wrong business entity. Give it as much thought and consideration as you did your initial preparations.

To aid you in this, we have provided two worksheets in Figures 5.3 and 5.4 on pages 59 and 60. They will help you assess your specific business needs as they pertain to which entity to start. Figure 5.3 allows you to list pluses and minuses for each type. Place specific emphasis on listing pluses and minuses relating to your specific business. Figure 5.4 lists the factors influencing your decision. List your company's needs and check which business form best provides those needs. When you are done, use these sheets to compare and contrast the entity types and decide which best provides for your business needs.

The choice of entity election for your small business depends on a variety of factors. These include your financial situation, technical needs, desired liability protection, and goals, as shown in Figure 5.2 on page 50.

Figure 5.2: **BUSINESS ENTITY SELECTION**

Some specific things to consider when selecting an entity type are:

1. Liability Needs

How much protection from the company's actions do you personally require? Does your form of business generally require liability protection?

2. Capital and Financial Requirements

How much capital do you have, and how much will you need over the next few years? How easily can you raise it under each of the entity types that follow?

3. Size

How big are you now, and how big do you plan to become? What entity fits your business size?

4. The Business You Are In

Certain businesses are best run under certain entity types. Does your business work best under a certain type?

5. Scope of Your Business Operation

Are you doing business locally, state-wide, or across state boundaries? What type of entity makes your business operation run best?

6. Short- and Long-Term Goals

What are your goals? How does each entity facilitate the fulfillment of those goals?

Much of your research and answers from the previous chapters can aid you in determining which type of business entity to elect. Keep in mind the six factors listed in Figure 5.2. The SBA's Small Business Startup Kits may help with this. Check for it on the SBA website. Finally, use the worksheets in Figures 5.3 and 5.4 to help you make your selection.

Sole Proprietorship

This is the simplest and most common form of business in America. There are an estimated sixteen-million-plus sole proprietors in the United States, and the number grows every year, especially with the surge in SOHO businesses. A sole proprietorship is not a legal entity like a corporation or limited liability company because the sole proprietor needs neither complex liability protection nor state licensing in order to operate. At most, a sole proprietor might need a local business license and must follow some withholding requirements. Simple as that.

Operating a sole proprietorship removes many of the burdensome government regulations from day-to-day considerations. Usually, the most intrusive thing is your yearly income taxes. It is you against the world, but not against a Goliath of government red tape. However, you must abide by any regulations that do affect you, so be aware of that.

Many small businesses and home-office businesses are sole proprietors because they do not yet need the protection afforded by incorporation or are too small to efficiently become a corporation. Sometimes they are sole proprietors because their goals are simple, thus eliminating the need to consider the effects of taxes or liability protection. Those with limited funds and limited goals (at least initially) may choose to become a sole proprietor first. Incorporation or partnership can wait until the company expands.

That's not to say all SOHO or microbusinesses are sole proprietors. If you need the liability protection, go with the corporation, the limited partnership, or the limited liability company.

We have listed some of the pluses and minuses of this simple yet effective business entity. You may come up with more relative to your business situation.

Pluses
- You get all the profits
- Easy to start: less paperwork to start it up and keep it running
- No legal help is needed to start it
- Income is taxed just once as personal income, thus eliminating complex tax forms
- Low start-up cost and often low operating costs
- You are the boss

• Many sole proprietors can operate their business from home
• Great for part-time businesses and SOHO businesses

Minuses
• You are personally liable for all business debts
• You also have unlimited legal liability
• All decisions and much of the work are on your shoulders, at least initially
• Growth and financial opportunities are limited
• It might be more expensive for things like health insurance
• You are limited in the amount of capital you will be able to receive
• The business ceases upon the death of the proprietor

In most states, becoming a sole proprietor is very easy. For example, in Indiana, a sole proprietor needs only register its name with the County Recorder's office if it does not contain the owner's name. That's it! Of course, there may be zoning requirements and some other considerations such as withholding and sales tax identification numbers, a Federal Employer Identification Number, and local and state regulations to follow. But on the whole, the sole proprietor is an excellent choice for certain SOHO, part-time, and/or microbusinesses. If your needs and goals are simple, this is the best way to start your business.

General Partnership

In a general partnership, two or more people create a for-profit, unincorporated business and are all part owners of it. In some ways, the general partnership is like a dual or multiperson sole proprietorship. Certainly, the usual requirements and rules governing each are somewhat similar.

Under a general partnership, both partners are equal partners in the venture and share the duties, responsibilities, revenue, and liabilities equally. Partnerships are affected by creating a partnership agreement, which is a simple contract between two or more people. It contains certain information that clarifies what the partnership is about: the partners, the responsibilities of each, the duration, the management, and financial arrangements.

Pluses
- Simple to start
- Like the sole proprietor, income is taxed as personal income
- Little regulation and start-up requirements
- Good for simple businesses or short-term business situations
- Potentially unlimited duration
- It may be easier to raise capital in a partnership than a sole proprietor

Minuses
- No liability protection for the partners
- The partners may eventually end up doing unequal amounts of the work
- Partnerships can lead to personal troubles between the partners
- Actions of one partner bind all partners to it
- If you need large amounts of capital or large businesses, you may want to become a corporation instead
- Partnership ends when one owner dies or leaves the company

Limited Partnership

The limited partnership is one in which there are two types of partners: general partners, who assume all responsibilities as owner and manager, and limited partners, who are limited in their liability to the amount he or she invested in the business. This form of business is affected in the same way as a general partnership, with one exception. The limited partnership is often required to register with the state government. Usually, a form is filled out and sent to the state for approval.

A partnership might choose to become a limited partnership depending on certain factors. Foremost would be the desire of one partner to supply capital, but not effort. That would be the limited partner. The remaining general partner(s) would be responsible for day-to-day operations and would assume the partnership's liability. If you do not wish to become a corporation or limited liability company but need to protect the liability of your investing partners, this is for you. Limited partnerships have more regulations and usually require state licensing, which sets them apart from general partnerships. Consult Chapter 13 for your state's limited partnership requirements.

Pluses
- The limited partners have liability protection
- Income is taxed as personal income only
- Potentially unlimited duration
- Good way to raise capital through limited partners
- Little government regulation

Minuses
- The general partners have no liability protection and do all of the work
- The partnership ends when one partner dies or leaves the company
- More state start-up requirements and regulations
- Limited partner can take his or her investment out of the company
- Limited partner may become disgruntled if the business is not run well

Limited Liability Company

Limited liability companies are newer business entities that are hybrids of limited partnerships and corporations. The limited liability company provides the best features of both, such as ease of formation, tax savings, and liability protection. These are fast becoming a very popular business election.

The limited liability corporation, or LLC, is basically a company with corporate liability protection and stockholding capabilities, and the tax advantages of a partnership or sole proprietor. The income of a limited liability company is taxed at the shareholder or owner level, thus eliminating the double taxation that occurs with corporations. However, the liability protection affords it the protection many small business owners desire. Recent laws have enabled them to obtain almost the same liability and tax protections as S-corporations, without certain corporation requirements and regulations. For small businesses that desire most of the benefits of incorporation, this is the way to go. An S-corp, mentioned later, is similar in function but more restrictive. You really have to look at your needs in order to choose between the two. Here is where an accountant or a lawyer can come be rather beneficial.

Pluses
- Income is taxed once
- Can have more than one class of stock
- Has unlimited liability protection, like corporations
- New laws enable this election to be basically a corporation with great tax benefits and stock regulations

Minuses
- Still not a corporation with the credibility offered by the "Inc." at the end of the business name
- May have a limited, rather than unlimited, life span; usually a set number of years, determined by the state
- This can be a tricky election
- May come under more IRS scrutiny

Becoming a limited liability company usually requires filing certain forms, much on the lines of a corporation. However, it can usually be done easily. Be sure to study your particular state's requirements before making the election.

Limited Liability Partnership

This is very similar to the LLC listed above. The difference is that it is a partnership with protection being afforded to the partners as one. As such, it does not offer the incentive of raising capital through stock. You will probably not use this election, but if you do, a section is listed in the next chapter on how to do it. A plus/minus section is not listed here. See the LLC plus/minus section for a similar list.

Corporation (C-Corp)

This is a for-profit organization created under the auspices of your state government. It is incorporated to do business within your state by an act of your state government. Millions of corporations dot the business landscape.

A corporation is owned by one or more people called stockholders, but those stockholders are separate from the company itself. That's to say they as stockholders have unlimited liability protection from the actions of the corporation. They cannot be held responsible for the actions of the corporation. That onus falls on the company executives and the company itself. Be aware of this fact before you make any decisions. The corporation offers legal protection for its owners, as they are separated from the company. This can be a consideration for those needing extra liability protection.

Because it is licensed to operate by state charter, the corporation is more regulated than most other forms of business entities. Start-up requirements usually include forms, fees, and stock certificates. However, the corporation offers distinct advantages, including better capital generation, stock, liability protection, unlimited life, and a professional name. And because of state recognition, the corporate "Inc." at the end of a name may be a psychological aid in company credibility. Many companies are incorporated in certain states for tax, regulation, and financial reasons. Two popular states for this are Nevada and Delaware. You will probably want to just stick with your own state. Here are some strengths and weaknesses of this election form.

Pluses
• Unlimited liability protection for stockholders
• Can offer more than one class of stock
• The "Inc." name may add credibility and professionalism to your business name
• Ability to grow is enhanced
• Raising capital is easier than in some other forms, such as sole proprietorships
• Hierarchy and structure may make duties within the corporation easier to define for partners starting a business

Minuses
• Income is taxed at the corporate and stockholder level
• Many ongoing state regulations and yearly requirements
• To do business in another state, you must file foreign corporation registrations with that state
• Company subjected to desires of a board of directors representing the stockholders
• Start-up is more lengthy and expensive than other elections

The election is accomplished by filing certain forms with your secretary of state. Additionally, yearly or biyearly requirements include such things as annual reports. Your state requirements will vary.

Most large companies are corporations primarily for the liability protection. You will make your election depending on your needs. However, you will want to at least investigate limited liability companies and S-corporations before making the regular corporation election. Either of the former will probably save you a great deal in tax savings.

Subchapter S-Corporation (S-Corp)

A special form of the corporation that you might try is the Subchapter S-corporation. This was created so as to give the owners of the corporation all the benefits (including limited liability) of the regular corporation, but without high corporate taxes. In some way, the limited liability company does a similar thing. S-corp income is reported on the owners' income taxes, thus reducing the amount of taxes paid and theoretically increasing profit.

An S-corp is a stock corporation licensed by a state as a corporation and classified by the IRS as a Subchapter S-corporation. This election is made by filing Form 2553 with the IRS. The S-corp can have seventy-five or fewer American stockholders holding one class of stock. It allows for the transfer of stock to family members and includes the prime incentive of single taxation on all company income.

Many businesses choose either the S-corp or the newer limited liability company when electing a business type. Ongoing changes in tax and regulatory laws affect all business entities, especially S-corps and limited liability companies. Keep abreast of current rules and regulations. They may have changed since publication.

Pluses
- Stockholders have liability protection for the actions of the company
- Income is taxed only once at the shareholder level
- Growth and raising capital is easier than certain other entity types
- Losses can be used to offset personal income
- Is basically a corporation but with better tax structure

Minuses
- Has only one class of stock
- Has many start-up requirements, including more federal requirements and potential state requirements
- May be under more IRS scrutiny
- Must adhere to strict fiscal guidelines
- Can only form one every five years

If you incorporate, you are a business of the state in which you incorporate. If you need to set up a store or do business in another state, that state will recognize you as a foreign corporation. States require incorporated businesses from other states to file forms in order to do business in that state. If you need to do business in another state, have your lawyer check the other state's laws first, and file any applicable forms. You can do this yourself but you may, at this stage in your growth, want to get a lawyer to make sure all requirements are met and to allow you to concentrate on running your business and making money.

These business entity types will no doubt change over the course of the years to come, but for now, they are the main types. Remember to carefully consider your election. This will affect your company for the next several years. Later, you can always become a different business entity, but you must check the rules and regulations before you do so.

Figure 5.3: BUSINESS TYPE ANALYSIS WORKSHEET

	Plus	Minus
Incorporation	1. 2. 3. 4. 5.	1. 2. 3. 4. 5.
Limited Liability Company	1. 2. 3. 4. 5.	1. 2. 3. 4. 5.
Limited Partnership	1. 2. 3. 4. 5.	1. 2. 3. 4. 5.
Sole Proprietor	1. 2. 3. 4. 5.	1. 2. 3. 4. 5.
Limited Liability Partnership	1. 2. 3. 4. 5.	1. 2. 3. 4. 5.
General Partnership	1. 2. 3. 4. 5.	1. 2. 3. 4. 5.
Other	1. 2. 3. 4. 5.	1. 2. 3. 4. 5.

Figure 5.4: **BUSINESS TYPE ELECTION WORKSHEET**

Fill out this sheet according to what is necessary for your business. Check off those entities that provide what you need.

Business Entity Types

Requirements	1 2 3 4 5 6 7
1._____	▢▢▢▢▢▢▢
2._____	▢▢▢▢▢▢▢
3._____	▢▢▢▢▢▢▢
4._____	▢▢▢▢▢▢▢
5._____	▢▢▢▢▢▢▢
6._____	▢▢▢▢▢▢▢
7._____	▢▢▢▢▢▢▢
8._____	▢▢▢▢▢▢▢
9._____	▢▢▢▢▢▢▢
10._____	▢▢▢▢▢▢▢
11._____	▢▢▢▢▢▢▢
12._____	▢▢▢▢▢▢▢
13._____	▢▢▢▢▢▢▢
14._____	▢▢▢▢▢▢▢
15._____	▢▢▢▢▢▢▢

1=Sole Proprietor 2=General Partnership 3=Limited Partnership 4=Limited Liability Company 5=Limited Liability Partnership 6=Corporation 7=S Corporation

Chapter

The Basics of Forming Each Type of Business Entity

▶ **The seven entities in detail**

▶ **Sole proprietorship**

▶ **General partnership**

▶ **Limited partnership**

▶ **Limited liability company**

▶ **Limited liability partnership**

▶ **Corporation (C-corp)**

▶ **Subchapter S-corporation (S-corp)**

By now, you should know with what business entity you want to structure your company. You answered the essential start-up questions and you wrote a great business plan. Now you can begin the process of actually starting the business. At this stage, you will be a few days or weeks away from actually being in business. Therefore, you want to make sure you are ready to enter into business. That is, is everything in order, and are you finally prepared to begin the actual work of your small business? If you are doing it part-time, are you ready for the extra hours (which you have been putting into doing your plan anyway)? If this is a full-time venture, make sure you have tied up any and all loose ends with your old job and that you have enough financial resources to last you through the start-up. The operative word here is *preparedness*. If you have been diligent, you are ready.

Each type of entity requires different processes, forms, fees, and regulations. Each takes different durations of time to form. Each has different ongoing requirements from either the state or federal governments. But basically, each is fairly easy to start. This chapter examines the requirements for each and just what it is like to go through the process. At this point, you might want to study Figure 6.2 on page 70 to brush up on the basic components of business start-up and entity election.

QUICK Tip

Do It Yourself: While many people use lawyers to incorporate, you may do it yourself. Also, a number of resources exist in the form of private companies and publications that show you how to incorporate yourself. Several are listed in Chapter 12.

For entities like corporations, partnerships, and limited liability companies, the requirements vary state-by-state. Some states have more requirements than others and charge more in the way of fees and taxes. By requesting and then reading literature from your secretary of state, you can better decide—with your lawyer, accountant, partner, SCORE officer, and/or your work from this book—what would be the best entity for you. Spend some time with Figure 6.1 on the next page, which lists the types of things all business owners, regardless of entity type, need to consider.

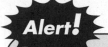

Choose Wisely: When starting a business, never go with the cheapest and easiest route simply for those reasons. If you need the legal protection of a limited liability company or even that of a corporation, go that route. Likewise, if you are starting a simple SOHO, you may be able to get away with being a sole proprietor or general partnership. Depending on your needs, you will enter into whatever form best suits your business. Our last advice here is again to be thorough in your selection process.

Figure 6.1: **ENTITY START-UP TIPS**

The following start-up tips are for all businesses at start-up and after. They are intended to save you money or time. Glance through to see which apply to you.

1. You will most likely need to file Form SS-4 Federal Employer Identification Number with the IRS. This can be done while you are forming your company. A sole proprietor may not need one of these. Consult the IRS for further information.

2. Consult an accountant and get advice on tax rules and filing information. A CPA working for him or herself is often a good bet because the service is more personal and professional.

3. Prepare your data in advance so it is handy for the lawyer. Include all relevant data, including company name and address, your name and address, the number and type of shares available, the purpose of the business, and the duration (usually perpetual). Use our worksheet "Vital Start-Up Information" on page 241 to do this.

4. You can save money by calling several lawyers to obtain a best price. Be sure to have the lawyer spell out exactly what services that includes. You can also call the Bar Association's lawyer referral service. It will vary, but in city like Fort Wayne, Indiana,it costs about $15.

continued

5. You can save on W-2 forms and the like by getting them directly from the IRS. Although they will probably give you only half a dozen, many small businesses do not need more than that, at least for the first year. After that, buy them in bulk at an office supply store.

6. Attend business workshops, seminars, and expositions in your area or state on a regular basis, before and after start-up. They can be invaluable for discovering business information, products, suppliers, and people.

7. Continuing education classes for adults at local, state, or community colleges or at technical schools can help you, partners, or employees learn current practices or brush up on past knowledge. Often, you do not need a previous college degree to attend.

8. Always keep records for at least five to eight years and keep your start-up records forever. We suggest, however, keeping all of your records permanently. Most small businesses will be able to find the space for the records, although every few years you may want to cull records you do not need.

9. You can always start as a sole proprietor or partnership and then incorporate as you get larger or your needs change.

10. For that professional look, no matter what business you'll start, use letterhead, business cards, and professional appearances in your business dealings. Sloth turns off customers and investors.

11. Check with local authorities for licenses and zoning information.

The Seven Entities in Detail

For a detailed description of numerous start-up considerations, review Figure 6.2 on page 70. With that said, let's examine how to start each of the seven entity types.

Sole proprietorship

All you need to do is become the business. You do not need to fill out legal forms of incorporation. There is no sole proprietor equivalent to the Articles of Incorporation or General Partnership Articles. However, there are certain state and local licensing documents and forms that may have to be completed. Obtain these at your county recorder's or applicable county/municipal office. Usually, this will be a business license, a required doing-business-as recording, or local licensing obligations. Other licenses may be required from your state for certain business activities or professions. You should contact the state to inquire about required state forms and/or professional or other licenses. Tax forms may need to be filed for withholding and sales tax. Again, you'll know if you need to file those.

We suggest that you go through the eight-step process described in Chapter 2 just as you would for a partnership or corporation. In fact, you will need to in order to complete your business plan and set up the financial arrangement for your business. You probably will need a sales tax identification number for retail and employer identification number as well.

Once you have set up your business, you can get an account at a bank for checking and other activities. Some very small businesses can simply use their own checking, but we advise looking into a separate checking account.

One final note: For most, including many SOHO businesses, this is the way to go, but think about it first. Remember you have all liability on your shoulders, including financial and legal. Still, this is the easiest and best route for most of you. You can always incorporate later, as your company grows.

General partnership

Like the sole proprietor, the general partnership is easy to enter into. Once again, you simply become the partnership. You and your partner will be general partners, each assuming a share of the risk and return and a share of the duties. An oral agreement is all that is needed, but a written agreement is practical, smart, and the only way to go. This way, you and your partner both agree to exactly the same terms and your signatures make it a contract. Be as concise and exact as possible, as a safeguard against possible problems later on. Include the partnership name, the partners, the responsibilities of each, the duration, the management, and financial arrangements, as well as any special sections you feel are necessary. Include complete details about each partner's duties and responsibilities. You might want to bullet them to make them stand out on the agreement. Have the agreement signatures notarized, and each person should keep an original copy of the instrument. If you have any questions, plunk down some money and talk with a lawyer about what to put into the agreement. Still, this is a basic form of business and you shouldn't have to see a lawyer. Just be concise and thorough in your partnership agreement.

Once you have your partnership agreement, file for a business license with your county recorder's office. Make sure you have any and all licenses needed. Check your local and state governments for these. After this, you may set up your checking account at a local bank. It is prudent to leave the finances to one of the partners, and this should be noted as part of the partnership agreement. But, both should be able to utilize checking accounts.

Remember, a periodic review of your partnership agreement and your business plan will ensure that your partnership is on the right track.

Limited partnership

The limited partnership starts the more complex start-up entities, although the processes are all very easy. Here, you have one or more general partners and one or more limited partners. States regulate limited partnerships more closely than general partnerships or sole proprietors. Thus, it is a good idea to contact your state for more information (forms, rules, codes) before talking to a lawyer.

To form a limited partnership, formulate and write a partnership agreement that clearly enumerates the same things for a general partnership as we listed in the section above and the role in the partnership of the limited partner(s).

Most states will require you to file a form called a limited partnership certificate or a certificate of limited partnership. Get this from a lawyer or the state, file it with the appropriate fee, and wait for the return certificate. Some states may require your partnership agreement be submitted with their forms. If so, simply comply.

Next, you will generally file for a business license at your county recorder's or clerk's office and apply for any other necessary state licenses. After this, you may set up your checking account at a local bank. Again, it is prudent to leave the finances to one of the partners, and this should be noted as part of the partnership agreement.

Limited liability company

The limited liability company is set up in similar fashion as the corporation.

Once ready, simply set up your structure of partners, investors, and officers. File the certificate of limited liability organization (name may vary), consent (certificate) of registered agent, and any trade name registration needed. These are filed with your secretary of state. Others may be necessary, depending on your state requirements.

The fees vary by state but are generally not too expensive. In Indiana, it costs about $110 to start up an LLC, and the fees will be higher or lower depending on your state's fees and requirements. Some states do not have a form per se but will provide a list of guidelines for inclusion in the articles of organization. Usually you will list the name of the company, the address, the name and address of the registered agent, the date the company is to dissolve, the names of the organizers or managers, and the rights the company will have. This is a vague template that your state may or may not follow. It is signed by the organizers and dated. The words "limited liability company" or "LLC" usually must be included in your company name.

When you write your state for forms, you will be given a list of fees and forms to file. Once these forms are submitted, you will receive a certification and can get your bank account and your business license at your county recorder's office. Again, be sure to check with your state or lawyer for any other licenses particular to your business or industry.

Limited liability partnership

The limited liability partnership is similar to the company, except it is a partnership. Where it exists, this entity is elected by filing the limited liability partnership certificate or selection. Again, this may not be a form, and you may have to create it yourself. Not all states have this election, so write to your state for more information. "LLP" or "Limited Liability Partnership" must generally appear in the name. After you start it, though, you can get your bank account, your county business license, and any other licenses.

Corporation (C-corp)

Incorporating is similar in process to forming a limited liability company, except most states have a simple one- or two-page form that you must fill out and submit. You can, under most circumstances, write your own articles if you wish to include more information than is included on the form. For most, the form that comes from the state will be enough. Most states have separate forms for regular and professional corporations.

Usually, your state form will ask you for the name of the corporation; the incorporators; the registered agent; the initial number of stock shares, their value, and their type; your duration (usually forever); the original company officers; and the purpose of your incorporation (what you are going to do).

Generally, if you are doing this yourself, you will first reserve a trade name, register your agent, and file the articles of incorporation. The state will return the forms as filed, and you may start business. You will need a corporate minutes book with stock certificates showing your initial shares and the value—use simple forms or go to an office stationery store for these. A shareholder's meeting must be held after you incorporate to elect officers of your board. That board must then meet for the first time to select bylaws. Since it is your company, you will most likely have the minutes and stock shares, so your first meeting should be quite easy. Remember to document the meeting, though; you are now a business and should conduct affairs accordingly.

QUICK Tip

Remember to Verify: The business entity selection conversation throughout this chapter outlines the typical start-up requirements for most states. States vary, though, so read your state's guidelines in the back of this book and write your state or get online to verify all important information.

These are generalized guidelines but are usually true for most states. Write your state for complete requirements.

If you are using an attorney to incorporate, you or your attorney will do all of this. Your signatures will be required on many of the forms. If more information is needed, your lawyer may write an article of incorporation himself or herself to include much more information that is pertinent to your wishes and your company's goals. The attorney will handle most of the requirements for you, but make sure to get in writing what services he or she will perform for what fee. The minimum is filing for a reserved name, filing your articles of incorporation, getting stock certificates, creating bylaws, and filing your federal identification numbers. Simply ask the attorney what the fee encompasses. Either way, you fill out, sign, and send your incorporation forms to the state.

You will also write your bylaws, as mentioned above. These are the codes, rules, and regulations used in the day-to-day operation—no matter the size of the company. They can be as complex as you wish; however, they should cover most contingencies that could affect your company. Often, a lawyer can do this for you in lieu of an initial stockholders' meeting, or can assist you. Operating under standard business codes, the requirements are straightforward and designed to keep your business running in a professional manner in compliance with laws and codes. These bylaws must be registered with the secretary of state.

Finally, professional business licenses from the state or state boards are usually required. You'll need to make sure you know if your business—or you personally—need to be licensed or bonded.

Subchapter S-corporation (S-corp)

For a Subchapter S-corporation, you will file your forms as described above. Some states may have slightly different forms. Generally, the only real difference is that you or your lawyer must file IRS Form 2553—Election by a Small Business Corporation—with the Internal Revenue Service. This states your legal right to become an S-corporation. After this, your only differences come in the number of stockholders and the annual tax returns. The S-corp will be required to file income tax returns for S-corporations. However, all income will be taxed at the shareholder level.

Figure 6.2: SPECIAL NOTES FOR START-UP BUSINESSES

- The address for the company can be your home if you follow zoning and IRS codes. Your home office should not be a place where customers come, unless you are zoned for business as well as residential.

- Any additional local or special state fees may also be required with regulatory licenses. To incorporate, a lawyer will cost between $400–$1000. Usually it is around $500. Tax number fees can cost more, as can other fees (incorporation, limited partnership, and stock fees).

- Self-incorporation forms can be obtained in a variety of paperback booklets and kits available at most nationwide chain bookstores or even business stationery stores. Check your local bookstores.

- For many entity types, franchise taxes, initial annual reports, securities filings, and Uniform Commercial Code filings may be required. These vary greatly from state to state. Our suggestion is to research every aspect of your state's requirements. Usually, the business or corporate section of your secretary of state's office will be able to help you.

- Remember that you are usually required to hold a Board of Director's meeting at least annually and to submit annual or biennial reports if you are a corporation or limited liability company. Again, know your state's requirements.

- For certain larger start-ups, avoiding lawyers will be extremely difficult for most people. They do, after all, handle incorporations all the time and will answer your questions. Most novice incorporators have dozens of questions, and the lawyer will be patient with you and answer them.

- New business entity forms are increasingly being created by state governments. During research on this edition, we ran into entities such as the business trust, co-ops, and limited liability limited partnerships while perusing state websites. Check your state or an attorney for information on new entities. Remember, not all states have all types of entities.

Chapter

Franchising: The Other Alternative

▶ **The ups and downs of franchising**

▶ **Franchises offer support**

▶ **Risks and returns**

At this point in the book, it is worthwhile to discuss franchising as an option for owning your own small business. You may be interested in buying a franchise, or you may eventually franchise your business as it grows and becomes successful.

Franchising is a business concept whereby a parent company uses affiliated owners to distribute or sell its products or services. It usually involves the parent company collecting an up-front licensing fee, an annual fee, and a percentage of the profit from the franchisee. In return, the franchisee gets to use the company name and the product or service, and participate in the collective advertising of the whole firm. Some franchises have more leeway in day-to-day operations and even in planning than others. It all depends on the franchiser and its business practices.

Starting up a franchise business can run the gamut from modest to costly. Some can be had for a few thousand dollars, but these are typically not location franchises, but rather business ideas and systems you run from your home or through mail order. Others are more involved, some costing several hundred thousand dollars to start. Many franchises work out deals with potential franchisees in order to finance the purchase of the franchise. The fees and costs to operate a franchise also vary greatly.

QUICK Tip

Franchising: A fast-growing segment of the American small business economy. In essence, owning a franchise is like owning a small business that's part of a big business. For instance, if you own one Subway sandwich franchise, you run it like a small business but are actually part of a giant network of other franchise locations and the corporate headquarters.

The Franchise Opportunities Handbook—published by the Department of Commerce—reports that franchising is equal to 33 percent of U.S. retail sales. The restaurant business is increasingly franchise-driven, which means more competition for local restaurants. What this means, of course, is that franchising as a whole is big business with a small business feel. With more and more products and services offered under the guise of franchises, it makes sense to talk about them as a viable small business option for you.

Everyone knows and uses franchised businesses. Some of them include Mail Boxes, Etc. mailing centers, The Glass Mechanix window repair system, car rental's Rent-A-Wreck, the copy center Sir Speedy Printer Center, fast food giants McDonald's and Pizza Hut, and auto repair/painters Midas and Maaco. Scores of other established and commonplace franchises operate across the nation, even in small towns and rural areas. Many small business publications have information and sometimes rankings of the best franchises. There is ample opportunity for the potential franchiser in this growing market segment if he or she has what it takes (and that includes money and determination).

The Ups and Downs of Franchising

Franchising may be an option for you if you are unsure about going it "alone" in business. But be aware that this is no easier a route than any of the other options. It takes long hours, a lot of money, and determination for the franchise to succeed. The only difference is the fact that the franchiser is behind you, which may eliminate some of the anxiety and uncertainty associated with starting a business. Some pluses and minuses are:

Pluses
- Combined advertising for the whole chain
- You start with everything: product/service, training, name recognition, and brands
- You are part of an established and most likely successful business network
- The company often provides technical advice and management-training programs

Minuses
- Can have a high start-up cost
- The legal and regulatory requirements are tremendous at start-up
- A franchise puts pressure on you to perform well for yourself and the parent company
- You are not a truly independent business; you might have to follow the parent company's pricing and product policies
- Can be expensive to run in terms of fees and percentages given to parent company

Small office or home office franchises exist, and their ads can be found in many small business magazines. Typically, these will be low-cost, less-profitable franchises. The franchiser may not be able to provide as much technical assistance and marketing prowess as the larger franchises. However, you may be able to start one part-time and then move to full-time. But be wary of anything that sounds too good to be true, especially if you go looking for a part-time SOHO franchise.

Franchises Offer Support

As listed in Figure 7.1, the parent company of a franchise should provide you with a few basic types of support and assistance. None of them are guaranteed, however. You must carefully analyze prospective franchises by reading the literature they send you and by asking questions of claims and statistics. If a franchiser does not supply you with everything the government publications recommend, ask for the missing information. This is one case where the government is on your side. Also, get everything in writing. Remember, this is your future, so take the time to think it out.

Risks and Returns

When you begin contemplating a franchise, the Department of Commerce recommends a list of guidelines to follow in order to evaluate the risk and returns of franchising. We've listed them here in Figure 7.2. In addition, several organizations and sources of information are available to the potential franchisee. A good government source is the Federal Trade Commission's guide to buying a franchise. It is a complete guide to the do's and don'ts. Also, your state government may regulate the sale of franchises, so you might want to investigate your state. The SBA may be able to help with some of its publications and with SCORE advice.

Two organizations that aid franchisees are the American Association of Franchisees and Dealers, and the International Franchise Association. These organizations can provide assistance, benefits, and networking opportunities. Many small business magazines or newspapers like *USA Today* and *Entrepreneur* devote copious space monthly to franchises and franchise news.

Figure 7.1: **FRANCHISE SUPPORT YOU CAN EXPECT**

When you look at a franchise, the franchiser (the company that licenses its product to you) should be willing to provide you with the following types of assistance at start-up and during the life of the franchise. These items should be clearly enumerated in the prospectus and in any contracts you sign:

1. Location analysis and counsel

2. Store development aid, including lease negotiation

3. Store design and equipment purchasing

4. Initial employee and management training, and continuing management counseling

5. Advertising and merchandising counsel and assistance

6. Standardized procedures and operations

7. Centralized purchasing with consequent savings

8. Financial assistance in the establishment of the business

(Source: *Franchise Opportunities Handbook*)

You can find the addresses, phone numbers, and/or Internet addresses of many of these sources of information on franchising in Chapter 12. Also, do not forget to talk to anyone you know who has purchased a franchise before. He or she will be able to tell you the road blocks and pitfalls to be aware of.

Buying a franchise begins with the eight Department of Commerce recommendations listed in Figure 7.1. Go through them with a lawyer so that you are 100 percent sure of each and every detail. Evaluate the market, yourself, the franchise, its claims, and the franchiser's representatives. Prepare your own business plan based on the one in this book, and be sure to ask yourself every conceivable question before entering into a franchise agreement. The plan will help you evaluate your goals and prepare you for your new business.

Figure 7.2: FRANCHISE START-UP PRECAUTIONS

This list is a general guide of considerations to bear in mind when considering franchise opportunities. Again, other publications and books will have more detailed information, and we urge you to consult them.

- Be aware of the risks. Like any business, there are good franchises and bad franchises. Take the time to find out which is which.

- Protect yourself by self-evaluation. Again, ask yourself whether you can handle the strains—financial, physical, mental—before you franchise.

- Protect yourself by investigating the franchise. Compare and contrast; talk to a variety of franchisers and franchisees.

- Protect yourself by studying disclosure statements. Here, the company should provide you with prospectuses or disclosure statements that contain information of several details of the franchise. Ask for one if they do not give you one. This is important.

- Protect yourself by checking out the disclosures. Field check the information in the disclosures by calling or visiting franchisees.

- Question earnings claims. Some states force franchisers to provide detailed information on this, some do not. This is the whole point of the business, so be careful.

- Obtain professional advice. This can be from government, industry, or individuals. The only thing that matters is that you do it. Talk to franchisers, franchisees, bankers, business leaders, lawyers, and accountants, just as for any other business option.

- As a potential franchisee, know your legal rights. Discuss this with a lawyer and consult the *Franchise Opportunities Handbook*, which is available from the U.S. Government Printing Office and other government resources.

The next step is to obtain the necessary financing and documentation to start the franchise. The documents vary as do the capital requirements. Again, you will need a lawyer to go over the documents, and they vary from franchise to franchise. It is important to remember not to rush into anything. Be sure of all the legal, accounting, tax, financial, and personal responsibilities you will have to yourself, the franchise store, and the parent company.

Franchising can be a wonderful, fulfilling career. It can lead to other businesses. If you are not purchasing one, you might think about franchising your own small business some day. It can also be financially successful for you, if you work at it. Just know the facts first.

Alert!

The Morning Paper: *USA Today* runs an Investment Opportunities page in the Money section every Wednesday. This contains companies advertising in the following areas: franchises, business opportunities, investment properties, business marketplace, and auctions. Several franchises are listed, from car painters and fast food to tax-preparation services and sports shops. Also visit it online at usatoday.franchisesolutions.com.

Chapter 8

Money: The Root of All Business

- ▶ **Finding and raising (and begging for) business capital**
- ▶ **Loans**
- ▶ **Networking**
- ▶ **The government**
- ▶ **Hard capital**
- ▶ **Getting creative**

Money is the root of all business. This is not a catchy phrase designed to get your attention. No matter what your other motivations, making money has to rank near the top of list of reasons to start a small business. If you understand this, you will also clearly understand that start-up capital is one of the most vital parts of your start-up. In order to properly start and run your business, you will need some amount of capital. The amount depends on your needs and your goals. Your business plan will contain this information. It is vital to properly capitalize your small business and to develop resources and methods to obtain further capital. A company without proper financing will have a tough time competing with established competitors. Additionally, a lack of capital will raise the risk of your business eventually closing or going bankrupt, neither of which you want. This chapter examines the many resources available to you in this quest. Other resources will be available in your local community or your state, so check around.

Finding and Raising (and Begging for) Business Capital

Basically, capital is money used to run your business. When you start your business, chances are your first source of capital will probably be your own wallet, savings account, or cashed-in insurance policy. Using your own savings is the simplest way to get start-up capital. You are the first (and maybe only) person to be interested in investing in this company you are founding. Therefore, you must be prepared to shell out your own hard-earned savings to help your business through its first few months, realizing that you could lose your money. If you are working part-time in your business, you may have income from your regular job that can be used for start-up costs and to help keep you afloat personally.

The following is a basic skeleton of the many places in which you can potentially obtain start-up capital, including loans, friends, partners, venture capitalists, and selling stock. Let's examine this complete listing.

Loans

Business loans

The bank is often the first place entrepreneurs think of when it comes to obtaining financing. While some banks offer loans to small businesses, some do not. It depends on the policy of the bank and the criteria they have established to loan money. Typically, a bank will loan money to a client if the client has collateral, has impeccable personal credit qualifications, or can repay the loan with ongoing income from something other than the start-up business.

The criteria banks will use to lend money are the amount and purpose of the loan, the primary and secondary sources of repaying the loan, the company data (such as management and operations), the financial data (including balance sheets and cash-flow statements), your personal credit history, and the reliability of the company. Any loan is usually secured by the equipment, personal or company assets, or the land being purchased. That does not stop most banks from wanting you to have full collateral.

Getting a loan at a bank is difficult; we'll tell you that up front. Most start-ups will not get them. However, if you can grow your business steadily over a period of time, banks will be more inclined to lend you money because you have proven you can operate your business. Many small business owners will simply have to grow their business first before approaching a bank. Smaller banks might be more apt to loan to a start-up or a SOHO business than a larger bank. Check local small banks for their policies.

Despite these facts, you may be able to get a loan. Some things to enhance your odds are to present yourself impeccably, be calm, answer questions honestly and directly, and have a killer business plan. Circumlocution, stammering, and lying are not things you want to do in front of the loan officer. Remember, too, that honesty is the best policy. If the bank turns you down, you can try another bank. Some first-time business start-ups have gone to several if not dozens of banks before getting a loan. Have patience.

If you qualify for a loan, you will want to know a few types of loan products banks offer. These can vary by bank or by region, but the basics are shown in Figure 8.1. Loans are typically paid for in installment payments or in balloon payments, which are a combination of installment loans with a final large payment. Some banks offer seasonal credit and bridge loans to cover specific periods in the business year.

Figure 8.1: **BANK FINANCING**

Banks can usually offer three general types of financing options. Study up on them before you go request financing from a bank. Here are some primary bank offerings:

---

1. Revolving lines of credit. Here you receive a line of credit payable over the course of, say, a year. Usually these are small amounts between $5,000 and $50,000. You generally can use the credit as you need it and are charged only on what you use.

2. Intermediate term debt. These shorter-term loans are usually sixty months or less in duration and they are secured by collateral such as equipment purchased. These are good ways to get equipment.

3. Term loans. These are used to generally acquire real estate and are typically amortized for up to 180-month periods. For small businesses, you will typically see loans up to the $100,000 mark.

A growing trend among larger banks is to offer businesses packages if they bank at that bank. These can include free checking, insurance, low minimum balances, ready lines of credit, ATM cards, credit cards, and being set up to accept Visa/MasterCard, either at your place of business or online, all without a lot of paperwork and complicated statements. For a SOHO business, something like this is a great way to start.

Also, some cities have bank pools in which many banks pool resources to offer loans to more risky small businesses. Often, your bank or your local economic development office can give you information on these programs. Loans under these programs typically have rates similar to bank rates, as opposed to SBA or other government-backed rates.

Personal loans

Another option is to get a loan in your name as opposed the business name—in other words, a personal loan. The most popular types of personal loans today are home equity loans and home equity lines of credit, both of which are based on the value of the equity you have in your home. Conventional installment loans are also available at local banks and credit unions of all sizes. While the interest rates are fixed with conventional installment loans, you are generally limited to five years in the length of the loan. Home equity loans, on the other hand, can have fixed terms up to thirty years.

Home equity loans

This may be a very valuable source of funding for your new small business. Home equity loans have several advantages over other types of financing. Here are some pluses and minuses:

Pluses
- Home equity loans are very common and widely available among financial institutions
- Your home is the collateral, so most homeowners will be accepted
- Not required to explain in detail your new business or business plan to the bank
- Interest is usually tax deductible; consult with your accountant or tax advisor regarding this potentially money-saving feature
- Most banks, large and small, offer home equity loans
- Maturity or length of loan can range between five to thirty years
- Many banks now offer an online application process. With all the other work involved in getting your business started, this may be an attractive convenience
- Fixed interest rate for length of loan

Minuses
- The idea of using your home can make some people nervous about this arrangement, however, using the equity in your home for debt consolidation, home improvements, or medical or education expenses often makes very good financial sense; using your home equity to start a new business is no different

- Limited to the amount of equity in your home; if you have not lived in your home for a long period of time, you may be unable to raise the amount of money you need from this source alone
- Some fees are involved, such as an appraisal to determine the value of your home and therefore the equity available

Home equity line of credit

Although a home equity line of credit provides many of the same advantages home equity loans do, they are different in a few important ways. First, the interest rate is not fixed and will change as market interest rates move up or down over time. They are usually pegged at a predetermined spread to the prime lending rate. Second, with a line of credit, you only pay interest on the amount of money you use, not the full line amount you have been approved for by the bank.

Pluses
- Home equity lines of credit are very common and widely available among financial institutions
- Your home is the collateral, so most homeowners will be accepted
- Not required to explain in detail your new business or business plan to the bank
- Interest is usually tax deductible; consult with your accountant or tax advisor regarding this potentially money-saving feature
- Most banks, large and small, offer home-equity lines
- Pay interest only on the amount you use
- Many banks now offer an online application process
- Variable interest rate, usually tied to the prime lending rate

Minuses
- Using your home as collateral for the loan
- Limited to the amount of equity in your home; if you have not lived in your home for a long period of time, you may be unable to raise the amount of money you need from this source alone
- Some fees are involved, such as an appraisal to determine the value of your home and therefore the equity available

Personal installment loans

Personal installment loans may be used in conjunction with other types or sources of capital-generating techniques. Since these loans are usually for more modest amounts of money and are usually required to be repaid within five years, other sources of capital will likely be required.

Pluses
- Usually easier to obtain than a small business loan
- Not required to explain in detail your new business or business plan to the bank
- Can use cars, boats, certificates of deposit, stocks, or other personal assets as collateral
- Available at all banks and credit unions
- Online application process available at most banks
- Fixed interest rate on loan

Minuses
- Limited borrowing ability
- Generally these loans are at higher interest rates
- Interest is not tax deductible

Networking

Friends and family

A small business often can raise money through friends and family, especially at start-up. Again, you should treat these people with professionalism by explaining the potential risks and returns.

When family and friends invest, they can be original stockholders or limited partners. Also, when you need more money or when you issue a direct public offering, they will be the first people you contact. If you run a SOHO business, this is an excellent source of start-up funds. Friends and family will be more likely to back you in one of these ventures than capitalists, the SBA, or bankers.

Another take on this source of financing is to tap into business colleagues or other businesspeople you may know, work with, or have networked with in the past.

Take on a partner

Taking in additional business partners either in the form of fellow incorporators or limited partners is another method of raising capital. Often, an investor will agree to become a limited partner on the strength of your plan and you personally. In this situation, your partner is strictly a financial backer. He or she will want to see a return on investment but will not want to participate in any of the work of the company. This can be an ideal situation if you do not want to sell stock or incorporate and if you have some backers already. Finding limited partners could be difficult, though, if you have to search for them. The laws of your state may not permit advertising, so you will have to network in order to find them. Often, these will be friends, family members, business associates, college friends, or others who have a professional or personal connection to you or any other principals in your company.

Business networking/brand name sharing

This is where one or more businesses combine to share one brand name, although each produces different goods. For example, let's say a group of automotive suppliers cannot get their products on shelves. They sign an agreement, put the common brand and logo on all products, and use a combined marketing/distribution system to place the goods. This really works and can increase each participating company's market share dramatically.

Although this is not capital per se, it is a way to get more out of your capital dollars and a way to raise your market share and product awareness. It is also a way to increase cash flow and revenues, which is one of the prime ways to attract traditional bank and SBA loans.

The Government

Small Business Administration

The federal government has a variety of departments and programs to aid small businesses, most notably through the Small Business Administration.

Additionally, as we mentioned earlier, it has some programs to aid minority- and women-owned small businesses. In addition to loans, it offers assistance in writing a business plan, financial accounting, management, manufacturing, retail, taxes, and other areas.

One unique and new source of SBA financial assistance is the Angel Capital Electronic Network—ACE-NET. This is an Internet-based program that allows cash-strapped, high-growth-potential businesses to "advertise" their companies to angel investors who sign up for the program. The angels invest in these companies, many too small for venture capital firms to touch.

The SBA operates a loan program for small business, including several different types of loans. Since the purpose of the SBA is to promote small businesses, it uses the loan program for that end. The SBA has a portfolio of $27 billion in loans to over 180,000 small businesses. It has guaranteed loans in which the SBA guarantees 75 to 90 percent of the loan you get from a bank and direct loans in which the SBA offers market rate loans for those unable to secure bank capital. A call or visit to an SBA office, Small Business Development Center, or SCORE office will expedite your search. The SBA also has loan application forms on its website for downloading. See Figure 8.2 for a complete list of these loan programs.

Figure 8.2: **SBA AS FINANCIER**

The following are some of the financing programs the SBA offers. Be sure to write or visit their website for complete information.

- SBA's 7(a) Loan Guarantee Program, which finances small businesses through a variety of specialized loan programs including LowDoc, Express, CAPLines, International Trade, Export Working Capital, Pollution Control, DELTA, Minority and Women's Prequal, Disabled Assistance, Qualified Employee Trusts, and Veteran's Loans. All of these can be further examined at the SBA website: www.sba.gov. Or write the SBA for information or go to a local SBA office.

- CAPLines loans are short-term, working-capital loans up to $750,000.

continued

- SBA's Microloan Program finances businesses through intermediaries, usually providing loans from $100 to $25,000. An ideal source for micro businesses or SOHO businesses without extravagant capital requirements.

- SBA's Certified Development Company (504 Loan) Program makes long-term loans for equipment and land, and for interest on an interim loan. Terms are up to twenty years with low down payments and 3 percent interest rates. These are often administered by or partnered with local government.

- The CAIP program provides assistance to locales that suffered job losses due to NAFTA. The SBA website has a list of communities that may participate.

- SBA's Small Business Investment Company Program is an amalgam of companies licensed and regulated by SBA that provide venture capital to start up a small business. These are located throughout the country.

- One-Stop Capital Shops gather local, state, and federal agencies in one location to address the financial needs of small businesses. There are locations in several states. Check your local SBA district office for information on SBA participation.

- Secondary Market and Surety Bond programs round out the list.

Grants/incentives

Sometimes foundations and government sources offer grants and incentives to small businesses. Local governments sometimes offer utility rate and property tax incentives for small businesses who employ locals. A city like Fort Wayne has a Community Development Corporation, which is charged with helping small businesses through programs, loans, enterprise zones, and assistance. See if your community has a similar agency. These agencies and programs can be a great source of information and capital.

Additionally, state and federal governments might offer tax benefits if you hire minorities, the disadvantaged, or teens during the summer. Check around. The Minority Business Development Agency was created to help minority businesses grow. It has nine regional centers. Anyone can benefit from locating in an Urban Enterprise Zone (UEZ), or a "brownfield." A brownfield is a tract of land that has been developed for industrial purposes and abandoned, and is usually located in disadvantaged parts of cities or blighted former industrial sites. Companies that set up shop there are offered tax incentives and government aid.

Also, minorities and women can benefit from grants issued by foundations and the government. Some grants come from specific groups as awards for entrepreneurship. Others come from groups dedicated to helping those in similar circumstances. Black, Hispanic, Asian, and women's groups abound. Simply check your local phone book for a list of supporting groups. Sometimes your local government can give you further information. Chapter 12 has resources as well.

Hard Capital

Venture capitalists

A venture capitalist is an individual or organization that invests in companies deemed worthy of growth and profitability. Steve Jobs got his start-up capital for the original Apple Computers from a venture capitalist. Typically, venture-capital firms will invest in a certain-sized company, usually one out of its start-up phase and well into its product's or service's expanding growth phase. The potential of rapid market growth for your company is the main criteria to receive capital from one of these sources.

Venture capitalists are professionals and not easily won over. In order to attract one and to sell your company's prospects, you have to be professional yourself. A venture capitalist will want to see your plan and your financials (balance sheets and cash-flow statements) and meet with you face-to-face. The capitalist will determine whether your company has a past record of success that will bring about a future record of growth. If your company fits this profile, you might attract a venture capitalist. Few start-ups will be financed this way, so the best route is to start your business, grow, and then prepare a proposal with an appropriate firm.

"Angel" investors

Like a venture capitalist, this person will invest in your company possibly for stock or a share in the company, certainly for profits. Angels can appear in any form—venture capitalists, friends, partners, family—and are generally swayed by the same professional standards that a venture capitalist is. However, some may be swayed for other reasons like friendship. Other angels will likely invest in growth-potential small companies that are overlooked by the much more stringent and expectant venture capitalists and venture capital firms. Hence the name "angels." One source of angel capital is the SBA's ACE-NET program listed on page 87.

QUICK Tip

Get Creative: You may be privy to other sources of capital, such as inheritance, stock, garage sale revenue, or rainy day money stuffed into a mason jar. We're getting pretty far-fetched here for a reason. We want you to search for capital in any and every avenue or venue possible. Do not overlook any potential legal source of capital.

You may be able to get these people to invest in your company on the later agreement that they will receive stock. For example, if you offer $1,000 investments, you can later promise to give one thousand shares of stock when you go public, or a certain percentage stake in the company. If you go this route, talk to a tax accountant for the federal tax consequences and an attorney for the legal requirements of your state.

Stock

Selling stock can bring capital to your company in the form of shareholder's equity. Stock is an issuance of ownership in a company. It is usually affected by a sale of a certificate for money to an individual or organization. When you start a corporation, you will have a certain number of shares issued at start-up. This might be all the capital you need. However, if you need more, you may have to make a public offering. This is where you go through an investment banker or brokerage to sell your stock to the public. This usually involves state and federal regulations, so in order to do it you should talk to a qualified accountant, lawyer, or banker. This can also be a costly route if you consider fees and percentage fees. Still, it is a viable and commonplace way to raise capital.

Another way is to offer a direct public offering (DPO). This is a stock offering that you offer "on your own" to the public without many of the associated banker/broker fees. Each state regulates this in different ways, so write to your state for information. If you receive approval from your state securities commission, you will be allowed to offer a set amount of DPO stock to the pubic. Most states will insist you set your stock price at $5 per share. Types of DPOs include SCOR (Small Corporate Offering Registration), which can raise up to $1,000,000; Regulation-A, under which you can sell up $5,000,000 in stock; and SB-2 offerings, which can raise up to $10,000,000. You will want to research these further with the help of a securities lawyer or an accountant. You will need them to assist you in filing as well.

Many investors will be wary of a start-up business, which is why you might have to wait until your company is making a steady cash flow and is growing before offering a DPO. And if you don't raise a minimum of the projected funds in a year, you must refund the money to investors. It boils down to risk and return.

Alert!

Reporting Your Progress: If you receive a bank loan or capital from other people, you must keep the bank or investors informed of your company's progress. A banker should see monthly financials, including your cash-flow statements, balance sheets, and receivables. Also, explain the things the loan is doing for your company in terms of inventory, marketing, personnel, capital purchases, and/or sales. The financials are more important, though. Your banker is, in essence, a partner who has a vested interest in your company. It is worth your while to work with him or her before, during, and after getting a loan.

Getting Creative

Part-time/seasonal job

A part-time job before, during, or after your start-up can provide capital and will be proof to potential investors and lenders that you are serious about financing your business. Although you will not raise a lot of money this way, it is a viable option, especially if you are starting a SOHO or microbusiness.

Use another business's assets

Maybe you have one part-time business with cash flow but limited growth opportunities. This business could provide eventual start-up capital for a future business with much more growth potential.

Barter

Business barter exchanges are relatively new and growing. Here you will exchange your goods or services for other goods and services with participating companies. You might sell your product for free accounting from an accountant or for auto work on your company vehicle from a garage. Many local exchanges have been set up. If your city has one, simply call up or drop by for some information.

The tax implications of a barter exchange are something to consider, as is the fact that you are not getting capital in the traditional sense. It is more like working capital in the form of goods/services received—virtual capital. Still, this can get you services and products that otherwise you'd have to part with capital to receive. It might cut into your profitability, but it will enable you to run your business with less start-up money.

Sell some of your assets

Some people sell lake cottages, homes, cars, furniture, stamp/coin collections, or other possessions to start their business. You will have to be careful because you don't want to sell something you'll want or need later on. The key here is to sell what you can, like a vacation home or a third car no one in the family is using.

If you have stock options at your current job or mutual funds, these can be sold to fund your new venture. It probably isn't prudent to dip into any IRAs for this purpose, though. Use your judgment. If you own another business, you might consider selling it in order to finance your new start-up.

Alert!

Stockholder Meetings: Send your stock investors annual reports at the end of the fiscal year. We suggest you provide quarterly or monthly updates as well, explaining what the company did the past month or months. Investors will appreciate these updates. Additionally, you are required to hold stockholder's meetings, which you should do on an annual basis. You will invite your investors to the meeting and discuss the company's progress thus far, vote on issues, and get a chance to talk face-to-face to your backers. Hold it on a Saturday so everyone can come.

If you are unable to raise capital, you might have to revise your business plan or put your venture on hold. Again, the best way to get money is to make some first. That is why most businesses must start small. Don't give up, though. Some companies have started small and grown huge and some have started big and failed. In essence, capital is very important, but must be used properly in conjunction with your plan and your goals.

Chapter

Unpleasant Business: Taxes and Insurance

- ▶ Social Security taxes
- ▶ Federal unemployment taxes
- ▶ Income withholding taxes
- ▶ Business income taxes
- ▶ Sales and use taxes
- ▶ Property taxes
- ▶ Inventory taxes
- ▶ Insurance

As they say, two things are certain in life—death and taxes. The latter is something you must come to grips with right away, and the former is dealt with through insurance. All fits in nicely, doesn't it? Well, it's not that simple, but you get the point.

Taxes and insurance can both heap burdensome costs upon your small business. Taxes are unavoidable. Insurance is trickier. You may or may not need certain types for your business and employees. This is where an accountant and especially an insurance agent come in handy to explain the particulars of taxes and insurance and the associated costs of each.

Taxes

The particulars of tax effects on small businesses is probably not lost on you. We mentioned earlier that taxes can affect your start-up entity election and are a great source of consternation to the small business owner. Every one has paid taxes before, but probably not like what you will pay while you run your small business. And paying them yourself makes you understand more fully the consequences of taxes on your bottom line. The basic taxes are shown in Figure 9.1on page 98.

In fact, most business owners cite regulations and taxes as being among the biggest hindrances to business. This is because both sap money and resources from your company. Although we could argue the fairness of taxing very small businesses at all (we feel there should be a minimum floor to reach before your small business is taxed), the fact is taxes are with us for good and we have to work with them.

QUICK Tip

Facing the Tax Burden: Taxes are a hassle, of course, but if you are diligent, you can make some of the tax laws and the deductions work for you. You will want to face them directly during your start-up research. Include your plan for dealing with taxes in your business plan and include them as costs of business.

Several things can affect your small business tax requirements. Your business entity type election will have the greatest effect. A corporation is taxed twice, while sole proprietorships, partnerships, limited liability companies, and S-corporations are taxed only once on earnings. A small business with employees will incur greater withholding, and the employer will be forced to pay a share of the employee's Social Security tax. Also, certain regulated businesses have fees and extra taxation to contend with, including special business licenses. State and local taxes and fees might include utility fees, property taxes, county and city taxes, and sales taxes. Here, the amount affecting your small business depends on whether you have property or an office/plant. Another consideration is the state you live in. All sales, property, and income taxes vary from state to state and from city to city. Additionally, some businesses incur greater tax and fee burdens than others. Larger firms incur more burdens than simple SOHO businesses.

An accountant will be able to tell you in advance of the many tax consequences of each business election, so be sure to consult one. Taxes affect your start-up because they will eat into your capital and will remain a fixed cost. It is also wise to hire an accountant to do your year-end taxes in order to provide you with the most deduction relief. Also, an accountant might be able to help you obtain tax relief through federal minority programs, certain employment programs, local economic development initiatives, and urban enterprise zones.

Social security taxes (FICA)

Anyone employing people is responsible for Social Security taxes. You even owe for yourself if you are self-employed (simply called the "self-employment tax"). The current tax rate is 7.65 percent for employees and the employer pays 7.65 percent. As your own employee, you will pay a 15.3 percent self-employed tax. Payment is due each quarter, unless you have over $5,000 of tax.

FICA tax has two parts: old age, survivors, and disability insurance (OASDI) and hospital insurance (HI), often just called Medicare. OASDI is 6.2 percent for the first $65,400 in wages and HI is 1.45 percent on all income (12.4 percent and 2.9 percent for self-employed). Most small businesses will pay quarterly returns, but some may have to pay monthly. A few small ones where the owner works on it part-time and does not take a paycheck may be responsible for only a yearly return on income at that time.

Figure 9.1: **FORMS OF TAXATION**

There are several basic types of taxes your business might incur. Study the rest of this chapter for a more in-depth discussion of each form of taxation.

Federal taxes include:

    Social Security taxes

    Federal unemployment taxes

    income withholding taxes

    business income taxes

State taxes include:

    income withholding taxes

    sales/use taxes

    business income taxes

Local taxes usually include:

    your property tax

    sometimes a county economic development tax or a city income tax

---

Federal unemployment taxes

"FUTA" comes from the Federal Unemployment Tax act. This tax is a quarterly tax for compensation to workers who have lost jobs for a variety of reasons. It is collected and then used in unemployment payments after an employee has been laid off. Its current rate is 6.2 percent and applies to the first $7,000 in wages you pay per year. After that, you have no further burden.

Additionally, your state may require you to file a report with it listing your tax liability. Contact your state for information on unemployment tax.

Income withholding taxes

Withholding is something we are all familiar with. If you employ people or pay yourself, you will be responsible for using government formulas to determine income withholding amounts on each paycheck. Partners, sole proprietors, limited liability company members, or shareholders may be required to pay quarterly estimated taxes to the government on Form 1040-ES. Other businesses such as corporations with many employees will pay quarterly withholding taxes on federal Form 941.

The current tax law has the following personal tax rates for 2002 and 2003: 10 percent, 27 percent, 30 percent, 35 percent, and 38.6 percent. The rates go down every year to 2006 to 10 percent, 25 percent, 28 percent, 33 percent, and 35 percent.

State and local income withholding taxes vary. New Hampshire pays nothing, while the rate in North Dakota is 12 percent. Other states fall somewhere in between. You will generally pay the same way as you do for federal taxes—quarterly with a "coupon" that you send to the state revenue department. Check your state revenue office for further information.

Business income taxes

Corporations are the only entity taxed twice, once at the corporate level and once at the stockholder's level. All other forms enjoy single taxation at the stockholder, partner, or owner level, usually paying a capital gains tax or a simple personal income tax. Much of this income is taxed as ordinary income and is done generally on either Form 1040 Schedule C or 1040 Schedule D. For instance, sole proprietors report income on their Form 1040 and on Schedule C or C-EZ. Partnerships report it on their 1040 and on Form 1065. Limited liability companies will report their business income on their regular income tax form and on Form 1065. Corporations will report income on Form 1120 or 1120A. S-corporations file it on Form 1120S. Federal corporate tax rates range from 15 percent to 35 percent. Chapter 13 has a complete list of corporate state tax rates.

Most states have income taxes for corporations, and some might for other entities such as partnerships and limited liability companies. These laws change constantly, so the best bet here is to contact your state for its requirements. You might want to call your state's Small Business Development Center for information as well.

Sales and use taxes

These are taxes on the sale of goods or services. Most will be state taxes, although some cities have sales taxes. You will need to collect sales tax depending on your state requirements (some states have no sales tax). Use taxes on out-of-state purchases used in your state are a further burden. Most states will require you to pay these use taxes in a similar manner to your sales taxes. Some states will also levy excise taxes on such things as sales of gasoline, liquor, and tobacco.

Sales taxes can be exempt on purchases you make with the intent of reselling the goods. The tax will be due when you sell the goods to the consumer. If you resell what you purchase, you will receive a sales tax exemption. You file for this number when you register your business with your revenue department. Most forms have check-off boxes allowing you to apply for a variety of taxes and for exemption. After you get the exemption, most states will have you fill out exempt forms every time you purchase goods this way. You give this form to the seller and pay no sales tax until you resell the goods.

QUICK Tip

Tax Payment: Most small businesses will pay monthly or quarterly estimated or actual sales tax, depending on sales volume and amount owed. The state will likely give you a "coupon" booklet or sheet with statements you fill out and submit with your check. More and more states are moving to electronic fund transfer to accomplish this.

Excise taxes are other forms of state taxes and will affect certain businesses, including wholesalers and retailers. Your state or SBDC can provide more information.

Property taxes

If you own your office or factory, you will naturally owe property taxes on your land and your plant/office. These vary from state to state. Most are paid to your county or township assessor's office either yearly or twice a year. Some are paid through mortgages.

Inventory taxes

One particularly heinous tax is the inventory tax. This is a tax due on your inventory of goods in, say, a warehouse or factory at a specific time of the year. You inventory your goods and then submit a form and a check to the state. The idea is to tax the goods you have yet to sell (or have not been able to sell). Brilliant, huh? Some states are doing away with these taxes, and we hope all will eventually.

The only good news for businesses is that during the nineties some states did away with inventory taxes, some sales taxes, lowered other sales tax rates, and lowered vehicle excise taxes and property taxes due to other sources of revenue, notably gaming and lottery proceeds. Still, the effect of taxation is great, and because of lower federal funding of certain state-managed programs at the start of the millennium, some states have had to look into raising taxes again, obliterating some of the lower taxes of the past decade.

To pay taxes, use the coupon booklets the federal government or your state sends you; also, many states give you the option to pay online through automated balance debiting. Regardless of method, you are still responsible to pay taxes. Talk to your accountant about this. Our state (Indiana) sent envelopes, forms, and explanations on state withholding when we formed our business. The federal government sent forms for quarterly taxes.

Most companies, except sole proprietorships, will file for a Federal Employer Identification Number (FEIN; IRS Form SS-4) that registers you with the IRS. Take your Federal ID number with you to register for state sales, excise, and withholding taxes. If you do not have it when you register, you may be able to send it to the state revenue office later. Check your state's requirements to see if the FEIN is even needed for state registration if you are a sole proprietor.

If you sell a good, you must record sales tax for the state in which the good is sold. If you sell via mail, collect only tax from residents of the state in which your business exists. Again, to purchase merchandise for resale, you will need a state sales tax exemption number. In some states, your sales tax number allows you to buy merchandise without paying sales tax. Once you resell it, you can collect the tax. In some states, when you collect sales tax, you keep a percentage because you are acting as the collection agent for that tax. This is not true in all cases, but in many. Consult your state for its requirements.

Remember, most taxes (social security, withholding) must be deposited quarterly if the total is $500 or more. In addition, Form 941 is filed for quarterly returns. Form 940 EZ or 940 will be sent for year-end FUTA tax returns, due January 31. W2s are due to the employee at the end of January, and the federal copy is due at the IRS on February 28. The states generally send simple forms and envelopes for withholding taxes and sales tax, although recently some have switched to an electronic transfer system for withholding over a certain amount. This money would be automatically transferred from your bank to the state. Your state may have a similar program.

Business tax returns, such as for income, are due within four months after the company's tax year ends. This is important to remember. If you do not get them by mid January, write for them, or better, go to your accountant. The following are some of the tax guides published by the IRS. We suggest you write the IRS to obtain all of them. Publication 15 (Circular E)—Employer's Tax Guide—is an excellent publication and is usually sent to the company. However, we suggest that you write the IRS for a copy while doing your research. In addition, call the IRS at 1-800-829-3676 for a copy of the *Small Business Resource Guide* on CD-ROM. It contains tax information, forms, and publications germane to small business. Figure 9.2 lists

---

Figure 9.2: IRS SMALL BUSINESS PUBLICATIONS

The following is a list of important individual IRS publications that will greatly help you understand all the important issues within small business taxation.

1 Your Rights as a Taxpayer

15 Circular E, Employer's Tax Guide (15A and 15B as well)

334 Tax Guide For Small Business

463 Travel, Entertainment, Gift, and Car Expenses

501 Exemptions, Standard Deduction, and Filing Information

502 Medical and Dental Expenses

505 Tax Withholding and Estimated Tax

509 Tax Calendars

510 Excise Taxes

529 Miscellaneous Deductions

533 Self-employment Tax

534 Depreciation

535 Business Expenses

536 Net Operating Losses

537 Installment Sales

538 Accounting Periods and Methods

541 Tax Information on Partnerships

542 Tax Information on Corporations

544 Sales and Other Dispositions of Assets

550 Investment Income and Expenses

552 Recordkeeping for Individuals

560 Retirement Plans for the Self-employed

575 Pension and Annuity Income

583 Starting a Business and Keeping Records

587 Business Use of Your Home

590 Individual Retirement Arrangements (IRAs)

594 The IRS Collection Process

724 Help Other People with Their Tax Returns

901 U.S. Tax Treaties

908 Bankruptcy and Tax Guide

910 Guide to Free Tax Services (contains a list of all publications)

911 Tax Information for Direct Sellers

1244 Employee's Daily Record of Tips

1518 Tax Calendar for Small Business

1544 Reporting Cash Payments of Over $10,000

some of the IRS publications important to small business owners.

Understanding taxes is one of the cornerstones of business success. Being unfamiliar with new tax laws, the numerous deductions, allowances, and so on, can cost you thousands of dollars over the years and many lost work hours. In order to take advantage of these great money-saving deductions and allowances, we suggest a competent tax accountant, reading books, studying deductions/allowances, and utilizing the existing IRS services.

Proper tax planning includes setting up the right business entity, using deductions, setting realistic goals, maintaining cash flow, and keeping expenses low. By making it a habit to read newspaper, magazine, and journal articles on taxes, you and your company stand a better chance of being abreast of tax changes. Changes in tax laws occur annually. Numerous books and software programs exist for tax preparation and information, some of which you will find listed in Chapter 12.

The SBA and IRS offer ways in which the entrepreneur can brush up on their tax knowledge. The SBA often holds seminars and the IRS has the Volunteer Income Tax Assistance. This program gives you the opportunity to keep current on tax regulations while helping others with their tax returns. IRS instructors teach you how to prepare such forms as the 1040EZ, 1040A, and the basic 1040 at no cost to you except your time. This is a great educational program.

Other IRS programs, often held at local offices, are geared toward specific business tax issues and are held throughout the year. A good place to check is the IRS website or your local IRS office.

Finally, most state departments of revenue hold tax seminars for new and growing businesses. Issues include payroll taxes, sales taxes, excise taxes, and franchise taxes, to name a few. These are low- or no-cost ways of educating yourself or your staff (if applicable) and keeping abreast of state tax laws and filing methods. These are often run by the SBA or the Small Business Development Centers, or the revenue field offices. Write your state revenue office for more information.

Finally, most states hold tax seminars for new and growing businesses. These are often run by the SBA or the Small Business Development Centers. Write your state revenue office for more information.

Figure 9.3: **EXPERT ACCOUNTING ADVICE**

An accountant will help you take advantage of the following full or partial tax deductions:

- Lawyer's fees against liability claims
- Accounting expenses for audits, bookkeeping, and tax-return preparation
- Business taxes, except federal income taxes, are deductible
- Cars used in the business (or your car if it is used for business)
- Bank account charges (for checking account)
- Charitable contributions
- Depreciation
- Repairs
- Insurance premiums
- Interest on business loans
- Business loses and bad debts
- Office rent
- Maintenance
- Salaries
- Merchandise costs
- Travel expenses when conducted for business
- Uniforms
- Social Security taxes paid by you for employees
- Office expenses and supplies
- Salaries
- Dues to business organizations
- Small business owner health insurance premiums

Insurance

Insurance is another matter to take seriously. For the new small office/home office company, the needs may be minimal. You may need insurance just for yourself or for inventory. However, larger small businesses may need a wide range of insurance covering inventory, liability, theft, employee health and life plans, and workers' compensation insurance. Many companies with full-time employees provide some semblance of health insurance and sick-time benefits. Often, this is a combination of employee and employer contributions on the insurance side.

The best thing to do in regard to insurance is talk with both your accountant and an insurance agent (or "shop" with several). Together, the three of you must determine what your needs will be, since needs vary between entities and in specific businesses. For example, two stores of similar nature may need different forms of insurance. Both will need insurance against theft, fire, or other damage to inventory or property, but one store may offer health insurance and the other not.

One main consideration for the start-up business is maintaining life and health insurance for yourself. If you have another job, you might be covered, or you could go onto your spouse's plan. When you plan for your business, you will have to come to terms with what insurance you personally need and what is needed by your business. We mentioned already that insurance needs vary by business, and that is true. The requirements of a SOHO business might be minimal compared to those of a manufacturing concern. However, a SOHO business involved in a profession like accounting might need liability insurance, and a small retail shop will need inventory and possibly business property insurance. With employees comes the added responsibilities of health and life insurance, unemployment taxes, and liability insurance.

The key with insurance is to be covered no matter what. No one likes making insurance payments, but there comes a time when some among us will say: I'm glad I did. We hope that's not you. Insurance needs are as varied as businesses, so consult a professional such as an accountant or insurance agent when you start your business. Don't get caught unaware.

Chapter  10

The Ties That Bind: Regulations and Licenses

▶ **Fair wages**

▶ **Equal opportunity/civil rights**

▶ **Worker safety**

▶ **Labor relations**

▶ **Fair treatment**

▶ **Benefits**

The previous chapter outlined the burden of taxes on small business. Regulations (and to a smaller extent, licensing requirements) are also part and parcel of external government influences and restrictions on small business. They have influence over how we employ workers, produce and sell goods, and develop companies. Most regulations were enacted to redress a real or perceived wrong, threat, or inequality. Over the years, a steady stream of government regulations has been enacted so that now literally hundreds if not thousands of local, state, and federal regulations face business owners.

Despite the overwhelming amount of regulations, they have in essence become a part of doing business like paying taxes and giving out sales receipts. They must be dealt with as a hindrance but not a blockage to doing business. If your company grows, sooner or later most simple regulations will cease to have a negative effect on the company. But that's when other regulations start affecting your business, and especially your employment and benefits practices. No one business can get around all regulations, but not all regulations apply to any one business. The key is to not panic but to deal with regulations in constructive ways.

Most small business owners would agree that government regulations are often the main cause of headaches for new businesspersons. There are local, state, and federal regulations that affect factors such as: employment, taxes, pollution, products, advertising, worker safety, prices, warranties, and communications. Most industries have industry-specific regulations to adhere to, many environmental in nature. Other regulations, like minimum wages, affect almost all employers, large and small. Your lawyer should inform you of those pertaining to your business. Local and state regulations are somewhat easier to deal with because your chance at redress is greater with local sources of regulations. Laws made in Washington are hard to argue about or discuss, but it is much easier to talk to local or state lawmakers and regulators. See Figure 10.1 for a quick run down of some of the regulations that should be familiar to you.

QUICK Tip

Mind Those Regulations: Many small business owners will face a simple set of regulations that are definitely surmountable. These include local zoning laws, start-up bureaucracy, and simple wage rules. Plan on dealing with these and other regulations before you start your business. Detail your strategies in either your business plan or in a separate, personal notebook. That way you can face them as they arise.

City and county zoning laws were created to keep residential, commercial, and industrial sites in specific areas of communities. When you start your business, you must adhere to these laws, especially if you have a home office. As long as you are not having clients over or are not creating too much business activity from your home office, you should be fine. If you need to use the office for more than paperwork, you can ask for a zoning variance from your local government.

Start-up bureaucracy includes the forms, rules, and fees you must pay to simply start business. The requirements vary depending on business entity type. Corporations are relatively complex and expensive to start compared to sole proprietors. Most of the regulations in starting a business have to do with liability protection, company officer registration, and capital (stocks). And the only real regulations here are registering everything in proper format with the proper fees.

Most small businesses will adhere to minimum wage laws and mandated Social Security benefits withholding. These are not so much a hindrance as a cost. Still, the minimum wage usually is between five and seven dollars, which should not break anyone's bank. Simply plan for the inclusion of each in your wage and benefit plan. Since size plays a big part in determining the amount of regulations affecting a business, many regulations like the Family and Medical Leave Act are valid only for businesses employing a certain number of people. Many small businesses will be unaffected by these acts. However, you should keep these and other regulations in mind as you plan future growth and then as you grow. You may choose to adhere to certain nonbinding regulations because of size; it might make good business sense to do so out of principle or for ethical reasons. This puts you in a good light with employees, the community, and customers.

Additionally, if you have employees, you must complete INS Form I-9 Employment Eligibility Verification for each employee. The IRS has the forms, and the purpose is to make sure that your employees are citizens or have the proper INS paperwork. In light of the rise of terrorism, regulations like these make sense, and more stringent regulations regarding alien workers/foreign workers may be forthcoming. Hiring employees also means Social Security regulations and withholding.

Along with regulations come licensing requirements. If you incorporate in any of the regulated professions, seek legal, governmental, and published sources of information before you incorporate. These professions include accountants, bankers, insurance, doctors and dentists, engineering, hotels, lawyers, real estate agents, liquor stores, teachers, detectives, and restaurants, just to name a tiny fraction. Be sure to check with your state department of commerce on your chosen field. Many require licenses or special testing in order to do business as a licensed professional. Professional engineers must pass a rigorous test in order to be called "professional engineers." Accountants must pass the Certified Public Accountant (CPA) test, which is also rigorous. Bars and often restaurants must obtain liquor licenses. Builders and contractors often must be bonded. Private investigators are licensed. Doctors are certified by state boards.

QUICK Tip

Check on Licensing: Licensing occurs at the state level and is usually handled by a state agency. Sometimes licenses are required at the city level, so check with the city clerk.

Figure 10.1: **IMPORTANT SMALL BUSINESS REGULATIONS TO CONSIDER**

These local, state, and federal regulations must all be taken into account whenever you plan a business. The more you understand and work with the regulations, the better your chances for success.

* The Federal Trade Commission Act (unfair trade)

* Fair Packaging and Labeling Act

* Mansion-Moss Warranty Act (a grand-daddy law that concerns warranties)

* UCC—the Uniform Commercial Code (sales contracts)

* Truth in Lending Act (disclosure of credit terms)

* Fair Credit Reporting Act (protection of personal credit)

In addition, as a prospective employer, you must be aware of the numerous laws that federal and state governments have passed regarding labor, safety, and a variety of other issues. There are taboos in many areas of employment such as discrimination and asking illegal questions in interviews. Knowing employment laws is as important as knowing tax laws. You do not want to get burned by accidentally breaking the law in your first time as a business owner.

Some regulations are nonenforceable and voluntary. These include joining the Better Business Bureau, the Chamber of Commerce, trade groups, or associations. Many of these have ethical tomes and requirements that businesses must follow in order to be a member in good standing.

We have listed some important regulations and laws you should know. Again, consult an attorney, the Chamber of Commerce, or your county law library for more in-depth treatment of regulatory laws, or call the agencies we list below. Like we said, some of these laws will not apply to all businesses, but they are all good ethical guides to follow. In fact, you might be able to include some of the concepts and ideas of regulations in your company or employee handbook. An employee handbook will be able to enumerate and detail the company's rules, ethics, and procedures. If you plan to hire employees, work on a handbook while writing your business plan. Also, see Figure 10.2 for a general snapshot of displaying regulations posters within the workplace.

Most employers will have to follow the FLSA act, the OSHA rules, the ERISA act provisions, and other regulations. All should follow fair employment practices.

Fair Wages

- Fair Labor Standards Act (FLSA). Sets the minimum wage at $5.15 an hour, provides for overtime pay past forty hours per week, and sets restrictions on child labor.
- Contract Work Hours and Safety Standards Act of 1962. Provides for time and a half paid for work over forty hours per week.
- Equal Pay Act of 1963. Prohibits discrimination in pay based on sex.
- Walsh-Healy Act. Sets minimum wages for federal contractors of $10,000 or over.
- Davis-Bacon Act. Minimum wage for federally funded projects of $2,000.

Equal Opportunity/Civil Rights

- Civil Rights Act of 1964. This makes it unlawful for employers with fifteen or more employees to discriminate against people based on race, color, religion, national origin, or sex in regards to hiring and employment.
- Age Discrimination in Employment Act of 1967. Prohibits firms with twenty or more employees from discriminating against workers forty or over.
- Equal Employment Opportunity Act of 1972. Prohibits firms with twenty or more employees from discriminating against them based on race, color, sex, national origin, or religion.
- Pregnancy Discrimination Act of 1978. Requires that pregnancy be treated just as other medical issues are treated.
- Rehabilitation Act of 1973. Prohibits discrimination against physically or mentally handicapped persons in federal contracts.

- Vietnam Era Veterans' Readjustment Assistance Act of 1974. Prohibits federal contractors with $10,000 of work from discriminating against Vietnam veterans.
- Immigration Reform and Control Act of 1986. Employers must verify proof of citizenship and legal residency in the United States of employees. Each employer must keep a completed federal I-9 form for each employee hired after 1986. This is an important business requirement.
- Americans with Disabilities Act of 1990. Prohibits employers with fifteen or more employees from discriminating against handicapped persons and requires them to provide accommodations that do not pose an undue hardship.
- Older Workers Benefit Protection Act of 1990. Prohibits discrimination with respect to employee benefits based on age, and regulates early retirement benefits.

Worker Safety

- Occupational Safety and Health Act of 1970 (OSHA). Employers must provide safe working conditions for workers. An addition to OSHA is the Hazard Communication Standard, which is a system of informing employees about hazards and how to respond to them.

Labor Relations

- National Labor Relations Act of 1935 (The Wagner Act). Gives employees the right to unionize.
- Taft-Hartley Act of 1947. Balances rights of employers and unions in relation to rights and negotiations.
- Landrum-Griffin Act of 1957. Gives rights to members within the union.

Fair Treatment

- Employee Polygraph Protection Act of 1988. Makes it unlawful for employers to request polygraph lie detector tests from employees or job applicants.

- Worker Adjustment and Retraining Notification Act of 1988 (WARN). States that employers must give sixty days warning if they plan to close the plant or lay off workers.
- Worker Compensation Laws. Laws are on the books from state to state. The requirements and benefits vary. Check your state for its worker compensation law.
- Whistleblower Protection Statutes of 1989. Protects employees of financial institutions and government contractors from retaliating against employees who report violations of the law.

Benefits

- Family and Medical Leave Act of 1991. Provides employees of companies with fifty or more employees up to twelve weeks of unpaid, and in some cases paid, leave to care for sick children, relatives, or themselves.
- Employee Retirement Income Security Act of 1974. Governs operation of pension and retirement benefits provided by private employers.

We should also mention the North American Free Trade Agreement (NAFTA). This agreement between the United States, Canada, and Mexico is designed to reduce or eliminate trade barriers between the member nations. These include tariffs and regulations. The idea is to create a friction-free flow of goods and services between the nations, benefiting each nation in turn. It has caused some companies to face new competition from abroad, while it has strengthened other companies. If you plan any exporting or importing, or any manufacturing, you might want to research NAFTA to see if it might affect you. Talk to an attorney, federal agencies (SBA, IRS), state agencies, or local chambers of commerce or think tanks.

As you can see, regulations can be sticky indeed, but if you keep current, you won't get hurt. Whatever you do, don't intentionally break the law just to make a few more dollars. It is not worth the fines, embarrassment, or even the loss of your company. Make the regulations work for you, and you will have eliminated one of the biggest headaches businesspeople face.

Figure 10.2: **MAKING COMPLIANCE PUBLIC**

Some of the regulations listed on pages 112–114 must be clearly posted in many places of employment. The minimum wage and the fair employment posters must generally be posted. In some states, others are mandatory. For example, North Dakota mandates that the following posters need to be prominently placed in the workplace:

- Federal and North Dakota Minimum Wage
- Workers Compensation Safety and Fraud Hotline
- Job Service North Dakota
- Employee Polygraph Protection Act
- Job Safety and Health Protection
- Equal Employment Opportunity Is the Law
- Family Medical Leave Act

Your state will have its own list. Again, many of these posters can be obtained at one of these numerous government regulatory bodies or through your state department of labor. Check around.

Agencies and Email Addresses:

- Department of Agriculture: www.usda.gov
- Department of Commerce: www.doc.gov
- Department of Labor: www.dol.gov
- Environmental Protection Agency: www.epa.gov
- Immigration and Naturalization Service: www.ins.usdoj.gov
- Internal Revenue Service: www.irs.ustreas.gov
- Securities and Exchange Commission: www.sec.gov

The SBA's website has some more information on regulations. Visit it at: www.sba.gov/ombudsman.

Figure 10.3: **REGULATIONS WORKSHEET**

Use this worksheet to list regulations you, your attorney, your accountant, or your advisor have determined relate to your business. Also list any special licenses you may need.

Regulations

1. _____
2. _____
3. _____
4. _____
5. _____
6. _____
7. _____
8. _____
9. _____
10. _____
11. _____
12. _____

Licenses Needed

1. _____
2. _____
3. _____
4. _____
5. _____
6. _____
7. _____
8. _____
9. _____

Planning for Tomorrow

▶ **The four keys to strategic planning**

▶ **Examining the strategic plan**

While many issues such as taxation, regulations, and business plans deal with start-up and beyond, most of our efforts in this book have dealt with start-up. Although that is the purpose of the book, the issue of strategic planning is so important to your post-start-up operations that we included a whole chapter on it. After your business is running, you will need to modify your initial business plan to meet your current needs. These needs could be growth, contraction, financial changes, or any other of a number of changes. At start-up, you need to keep the big picture of economic changes in mind and their potential effect on your business.

The Four Keys to Strategic Planning

This chapter is designed to introduce you to the concept of strategic planning and to present the many ways planning can help business growth and profitability. More worldwide competition, cheaper labor markets, and higher numbers of entrepreneurs starting their own businesses all affect the climate in which you operate. These pressures need to be addressed if your business is to survive. By regularly addressing them, you will learn to apply proactive and creative solutions to current and upcoming problems. That is the real beauty of strategic planning: it allows you to *plan* the future. The point here is that you do not want to be eighty years old and still mumbling about what could or should have been. Strategic planning will enable you to do what needs to be done.

Strategic planning is simply the ongoing process of planning for your small business. In one way or another, every business must undergo strategic planning, regardless of size. Its importance becomes clear once the outside pressures on your business begin to become apparent and the lessons of running a business are learned. Your initial business plan was meant to get your business started and to act as a template for future growth—two, three, and five years from now, and beyond. That initial template may be fine in a general or macro sense, but on the specific or micro level, it will need tweaking. That is where the concept of planning comes into play. Planning will tell you what is right and what is wrong with your small business.

You will learn to recognize those parts of your plan (and goals) that are not working or were unrealistic in the first place. You will certainly come across areas that have either failed to produce the desired results, or simply need updating to meet the current state of your business, the economy, or your goals. That's perfectly healthy in a business, but the key is to minimize your weaknesses.

Planning will also highlight your successes and benefit your understanding of what you are doing right. An important part of the ongoing strategic planning is recognizing your strengths and enhancing them. After all, any strength or expertise that becomes apparent is beneficial to your company. You will want to concentrate on exploiting these strengths.

A strategic plan also enables you to review your short- and long-term goals and understand if these are still realistic milestones to strive for. Sometimes they must be revised, changed, or eliminated. By planning, you can determine what goals need refinement or elimination. Planning allows you the choice of determining how you will reach these goals based on your current and future business status. It also forces you to examine why those goals were unreachable or why you achieved them.

As we mentioned earlier, all businesses should conduct strategic planning at least once a year. SOHO businesses can use strategic planning sessions in order to facilitate growth, evaluate the benefits of the home office, and identify changes or obstacles in the environment. For instance, having a home office is stressful because family and personal life occurs everywhere around the office, so you might revise your plan to move into a separate office. Or you may recognize a problem such as a stressed home office and still decide to do nothing about it. In planning, you get that choice. Not every problem needs to be addressed, because problems are relative, and their importance to your operations may not warrant any immediate action. When you complete your planning sessions, you will be able to tell where your efforts should be expended.

Figure 11.1: **THE FOUR KEYS TO STRATEGIC PLANNING**

There are four keys to strategic planning:

Recognition
Formulation
Implementation
Evaluation

The first step is recognizing what happened to your company in the past six months to a year. The second is formulating strategies to enhance your progress and address your problems. Next, you will implement strategies and objectives meant to achieve new and existing goals. Finally, you evaluate (within a year) the results of your new strategies.

Sometimes you have to review your progress monthly or quarterly. That's fine. You can fine-tune or adjust your business plan at those times. Also, you can get an earlier glimpse of the success or failure of your strategies. Again, you will be the one to determine when and how you review your strategy implementation.

Figure 11.1 examines a typical strategic plan. It is used to determine your strengths and weaknesses, opportunities and threats, and formulate actions meant to enhance or nullify them respectively. After you have gone through your initial planning session, you can then use the new strategic plan to rewrite or revise your current business plan. This is useful, especially if you plan growth and need financing. The strategic plan can aid and enhance the business plan, making the chances of security financing all the better.

At the end of every year, perform a strategic evaluation of your company. If your company is small, the whole staff will probably be involved. If you have grown, the board of directors and top management will want to perform this duty jointly.

Figure 11.2: STRATEGIC PLAN OUTLINE

We suggest the following course of action for developing a strategic business plan for your company. For each section, complete the information as best you can using all resources available to you. This will take some time, so do not try and rush through.

Strategic Planning Outline

I. Introduction
- Introduction
- Issues Pertaining to Your Company
- Mission Statement
- Current Objectives

II. Strengths of Your Company
- Management and Operations
- Marketing
- Finance and Accounting

III. Weaknesses of Your Company
- Management and Operations
- Marketing
- Finance and Accounting

IV. Analysis
- Competitor Analysis
- Key Ingredients Matrix
- Opportunities for Your Company
- Threats to Your Company

V. New Strategic Plan
- Redefined Mission Statement
- New Company Objectives
- Possible Strategies
- Chosen Strategies
- Implementation of Chosen Strategies
- Strategic Evaluation

VI. Appendices, Bibliography, Indices

Examining the Strategic Plan

Now let's examine each section of this sample strategic plan. At the end of this chapter is a list of SBA publications that might assist you further. One thing to remember is to use this strategic plan to review the work you have done this year and to plan for next year. A plan can help you determine your needs in all areas, including finance. Once this plan is in place, you might decide to pursue a loan after or make a stock offering. Maybe you will decide to grow or expand into different areas. Whatever you decide, remember that your plan will guide you for the next year or so.

QUICK Tip

Keeping Ahead: The best way to stay abreast of current and future trends is to order your competitors' catalogs and products, or try their services on a periodic basis. You'll also need to continuously monitor domestic and foreign events through news magazines, newspapers, and television.

Introduction

This is the front material for your plan, and should be completed with as much care as the other four parts of your strategic plan. They will be used to determine new objectives and mission statements.

- Introduction. Briefly describe your company. Since the strategic plan is for you, do not include all of the information you already know; instead, you should be covering those things that have changed since your first business plan.

- Issues pertaining to your company. List those economic, political, and social issues at the moment that affect your company directly.

- Mission statement. Write your original mission statement here as a reminder of your basic goals. You might revise it later.

- Current objectives. What are your objectives or goals now? In other words, list your objectives when you wrote your first business plan.

Strengths of your company

Here you will make lists of the positive things that happened to you this year. Your strengths will be self-evident, but listing them will help later when you determine new goals and strategies.

- Management and operations. Where, what, and who are your strengths in your company's management? List the things you did right this year. Remember, this strategic plan is for *you*. Be honest and do not build up your management style or your operations.
- Marketing. Where and what are your marketing strengths? What worked this year? What were the reasons you sold well? What advertising and distribution systems do you credit?
- Finance and accounting. Where and what are your finance/accounting strengths? How did you use your capital to generate business?

Weaknesses of your company

This section is similar to the previous one except it lists your weaknesses. These are areas where you recognize what was deficient in your past year and where you need to improve. Weaknesses are important to note because they are the prime areas you will want to strengthen and improve.

- Management and operations. Where, what, and who are your weaknesses in running the company? Why are these weaknesses? Are you able to keep up with demand?
- Marketing. Where and what are your marketing weaknesses? What marketing/advertising did not work? How did your distribution channels suit your business?
- Finance and accounting. Where and what are your finance/accounting weaknesses? If you needed more capital, note it here. Do your credit policies work? Is there a constant cash flow?

QUICK Tip

Useful Resources: SBA publication MP 21, Developing a Strategic Business Plan, will also be of valued help, as will EB06, Strategic Planning for Growing Businesses. The next chapter deals with these and other resources.

Analysis

This section analyzes your competitors and how your business stacks up against them. You need to be thorough and honest because you will use the ideas you generate along with parts of the analysis to determine if you need to consider new strategies.

- Competitor analysis. Who are your competitors and how are they doing? Did they succeed last year? Did they cost you business?
- Key ingredients matrix. What are the key ingredients for success in your business? List as many factors you can think of. On page 126–127, you will use these key ingredients in conjunction with your upcoming SWOT (Strength/Weaknesses/Opportunities/Threats) analysis to determine how to take advantage of them to make your company successful.
- Opportunities for your company. Name opportunities forecasted and reported in various business and news magazines, journals, and programs. These can come from external sources and from inside your company. Anything that could help your company should be listed.
- Threats to your company. Name events that could threaten or harm your company from various business and news magazines, journals, and programs. Threats are internal and external. They threaten to reduce sales, profitability, growth, or production.

Alert!

SWOT Analysis: In a small business atmosphere, your strength will lie in being able to assess your own strengths and weaknesses. You can do this through a SWOT analysis.

Strengths

Weaknesses

Opportunities

Threats

New strategic plan

Finally, all of the previous analyses come together in this final section to form a cohesive strategic plan. First, you will want to compare your strengths and weaknesses alongside your opportunities and threats. This is your SWOT analysis. Next, identify those key ingredients for success that can be maximized by your strengths and opportunities. Then list your weaknesses and threats and how your strengths and opportunities can help overcome them. Finally, you will want to pick out those areas you specifically want to improve on next year. You do not have to select everything. This will form the basis of your new plan.

• New company objectives. If you need new objectives, formulate them. These new objectives are based on your past objectives and what your SWOT analysis tells you what you need to do next year to improve your business.

• Possible strategies. List as many possible strategies to improve your company as you can think of. Keep in mind that you want to maximize your strengths/opportunities and minimize your weaknesses/threats. Formulate strategies appropriately.

• Chosen strategies. Choose the strategies that you feel will best create the desired outcome and meet the new objectives. Choose only those you can implement. Some may have to wait until next year. The most urgent needs should be addressed first.

• Redefined mission statement. If you need a new mission statement after this analysis, write one. Most likely, you will want to enhance the previous one.

• Implementation of chosen strategies. How will you implement the strategies? Make a listing of the ways your strategies can be worked into your operations within your budget. If you are seeking more capital, note this.

• Strategic evaluation. Determine how, over a period of time, you will measure and evaluate the success or failure of your chosen strategies. Once you determine a monthly, quarterly, or yearly evaluation timetable, stick to it.

Appendices, bibliography, and indices

This is an optional section to use if you generate supporting documents while working on your strategic plan. If you have an elaborate strategic planning session, you may use this area to file your supporting research and materials.

As you can see, a strategic plan allows you to continuously analyze, update, and revise your two- to five-year business strategy to incorporate changing circumstances, products, or economic forces. This is very, very important. Businesses often fail, and fail miserably, because of their own shortcomings in the planning department. Even in times of success, you must continuously look over the horizon for future opportunities and threats, and behind your back at what your competitors are doing. Remember: Recognize, Formulate, Implement, and Evaluate.

Chapter

Resources, Resources

▶ **Books**

▶ **Government sources**

▶ **Internet**

▶ **Media**

▶ **Organizations and groups**

▶ **Periodic Publications**

▶ **Services**

▶ **Suppliers**

This final chapter was written to inform you of the wide variety of sources of help—publications, services, software, government assistance, supplies, and suppliers. You will want to use this chapter's resources in conjunction with many of the other chapters in this book.

Fortunately, we live in the information age. This enables you to obtain more information on starting a business—and from a greater variety of sources—than anyone at any other time in our history, and the future looks even brighter. The key to a successful business idea, business plan, and business start-up is *information*. Only a strong foundation of information will allow you to grow into the company that your dreams first foresaw and your goals envision.

This compendium of resources will be invaluable in your research and in the operation of your small business. We have included government agencies, individuals, and companies we feel might be of use to you. These sources can supply books, information, publications, supplies, advice, news, and statistics. Some, like the Small Business Administration, have publications for sale at little or moderate cost; others, like the Internal Revenue Service, offer their information for free. Technical and expert advice and help is available from numerous government and private-sector sources. Some of these have their own websites. Others are business suppliers who can provide forms, software, computers, and the like.

Regardless of your business size or entity, many of these resources can be of great value to you. We especially like the Internet, because one business site often links you to others. For example, the SBA site links to dozens of other government and private websites. We encourage the use of any and all free information on the Internet because that simply saves you money. However, be sure to double check all information you receive online; some sources can be deemed reliable while others will need you to back them up with further research.

We have organized the listings into categories depending on what resources they typically supply. Again, some categories will overlap. While this list is by no means exhaustive, it is a good guide of sources available to you.

Books

- *Business Building Ideas for Franchises and Small Business.* This booklet has ideas and suggestions on promoting your small business. The book is listed on the website www.enterpriseworksinc.org, and may be available from them.
- *Buying Your First Franchise.* This book contains information that will assist you in selecting your franchise in an educated and informed manner. Cost is $13.00. To order, call 1-800-543-1038 or visit the website at www.franchise.org.
- *Franchise Opportunities Guide.* This is a guide from the IFA on franchises available for operation. Cost is $17.00. To order, call 1-800-543-1038 or visit the website at www.franchise.org.
- *How to Get a Small Business Loan* by Bryan Milling. A comprehensive look at a variety of loan resources, application processes, and helpful information on how loan programs work. The information in this book is from a banker's prospective, telling you what he wants from your loan proposals/applications. It will prove very useful for your business no matter what stage it is in. Available at bookstores, on the Web, or call 1-800-432-7444.
- *Info Power III* and *Government Giveaways for Entrepreneurs* by Matthew Lesko. These books from Info USA Inc. contain information that might be of great value to you, though not in a start-up way, but more in a resource-finding capacity. Available at bookstores, libraries, and at www.matthewlesko books.com.
- *The SBA Loan Book* by Charles H. Gree. Published by Adams Media, this book details the processes for securing SBA loans and provides valuable insight into enhancing your ability to get a loan by revealing the secrets and the do's and don'ts of SBA loan applications.
- *Small Business for Dummies* by Eric Tyson and Jim Schell. Another of the Dummies books, this one focusing on the small business.
- *The Small Business Handbook* by Irving Burstiner. An excellent book for the first timer. Ask your librarian or bookseller if they have a copy or call or write to Prentice Hall Press to see if it is still in stock.
- *Start Smart: Your Home-Based Business* by Bernadette Tiernan. A guide for the home based business with information relevant to those specific start-ups.

- *Streetwise Small Business Start-Up* by Bob Adams. This book has loads of information on start-ups from a master of small business, Bob Adams.
- *Your First Business Plan* by Joseph Covello & Brian Hazelgren. This is a great book on writing a business plan.

Government Sources

- Consumer Information Center. Provides a catalog of free or cheap consumer federal publications. Some can aid your small business. www.pueblo.gsa.gov
  CIC
  P.O. Box WWW
  Pueblo, CO 81009
- Copyrights. These protect written documents against exploitation. If you produce written materials, art works, or programs, you will need this information. Write:
  Library of Congress
  Copyright Office
  101 Independence Ave. S.E.
  Washington, DC 20559-6000
- Department of Commerce. The commerce department has a Business Assistance Center and offers information. www.doc.gov
- Department of Labor. The DOL has publications on compliance with labor laws and the notable Small Business Handbook. Visit the website at www.dol.gov or write:
  Department of Labor
  200 Constitution Avenue, NW
  Washington, DC 20210
- Federal Trade Commission. This organization has over one hundred free publications on consumer and business topics, including the Consumer Guide to Buying a Franchise. The best way to access these is by visiting www.ftc.gov.
- Government auctions are excellent ways to get furniture and equipment. Local and federal agencies hold auctions; check your local newspaper for information.

- Government Printing Office. This office handles federal documents and publications and has a wealth of information on hundreds of topics from agriculture to business to history. The best way to get information is to visit the website at www.gpo.gov.
- Internal Revenue Service. The IRS has dozens of publications. Be sure to get the Tax Guide for Small Business. For more information, visit the website www.irs.ustreas.gov. The IRS also offers local services like tax seminars and aid programs. Write to:

  IRS

  Washington, DC 20224
- Library. Of course, you say. But the library is an excellent source of free resources and publications. The librarian will also be able to assist you in your searches. Your local library should have a business section that will contain guides to such things as trade associations, other companies, services, government information, statistical data, and phone books from other parts of the country.
- Local Government. Your local county or city government will likely have an economic development office where local assistance and certain SBA loans can be obtained. Most cities will have local loan, grant, or tax abatement programs such as the Urban Enterprise Zone initiatives.
- Minority Business Development Agency. This is the only federal agency created to encourage minority ownership of small businesses. It coordinates federal programs, collects information and dispenses it, and funds training assistance for minorities at nine regional sites in Atlanta, Miami, Chicago, Dallas, New York, Boston, Philadelphia, San Francisco, and Los Angeles. For further information, visit the MBDA website at www.mbda.gov.
- Small Business Administration. The SBA is specifically geared toward encouraging small business growth and will provide you with most of your information, at least initially. The SBA has publications, videos, software, programs, loans, and websites. The publications, software, and videos are listed in the appendix. The SBA's Small Business Development Centers are located in every state and provide management assistance to current and potential small business owners. Its Business Information Centers are government/private ventures providing high-tech software

and an array of counseling services and training to small businesses. SBA field offices are in every major city, as are Service Corps of Retired Executive Centers, which provide small business owners assistance from retired executives and businesspeople. See your state requirements for locations. Also, be sure to get the Small Business Startup Kit from the SBA. It's loaded with important information on business start-ups. The SBA National Ombudsman is at 1-888-734-3247 or visit the website at www.sba.gov/ombudsman. Call the SBA Answer Desk at 1-800-8-ASK-SBA or visit the SBA website at www.sba.gov. The address is:

SBA Answer Desk
6302 Fairview Road, Suite 300
Charlotte, NC 28210

- State governments. Like local governments, states often have their own economic development departments or departments of commerce. These can be treasure troves of booklets, pamphlets, and other information on starting small businesses. Check your state section in your phone book.

- Trademarks and patents. To protect your trademark on your product or service, contact your state trademark agency and also the federal government, which registers the trademark before the state does. Request patent and trademark information at:

General Information Services Division
US Patent & Trademark Office
Crystal Plaza 3, Room 2C02
Washington, DC 20231
Phone: 1-800-786-9199

- The U.S. government maintains bookstores in several major cities; these contain publications from the government available to the public for sale. See "Government Printing Office" on page 133 for the online bookstore.

Internet

- Amazon.com. This is the first place to search for books online. Amazon has hundreds of business titles and business magazines, and it's easy to search for books by category.

- Bloomberg.com. One of the top-rated financial sites on the Web. It is a great place to follow financial markets, the economy, and interest rates.

- Business.com. This site is a search engine for business-related websites, and thus business books and information.

- Business Advisor Site. This site will link you with all government websites and has a host of its own information. It is located at www.business.gov.

- Business Nation. This site features a vast array of links to other business and government sites. It's a good way to search for state-by-state help from one resource. It is located at www.businessnation.com.

- CFO.com. This site features articles from CFO magazine and is useful for keeping abreast of all matters relating to the financial management of any business. Areas of focus include accounting, tax, capital markets, e-commerce, human resources/benefits, and hardware issues, along with top news stories.

- Enterprise Works. This site is devoted to helping clients build small businesses. Contact them for information by first visiting the website at www.enterpriseworksinc.org.

- First Gov. Www.firstgov.gov is an omnibus website with links to other government sites. It acts as a portal to make surfing for government information easier, and is invaluable for research.

- Government Information Exchange. Run by the Consumer Information Center, www.info.gov has some great government information and links to other sites.

- Hallsmallbusiness.com. This site has a huge selection of business books and publications for sale. Some of the books we mention are available there.

- Income Opportunities (www.incomeops.com) has a variety of start-up, Internet, and home business information and publications.

- Institute of Management and Administration (www.ioma.com) is a website containing e-newsletter listings, business reports, and a management library for research. Note that there is a cost to do certain research, but it might be worth it.

- ISBC. The International Small Business Consortium (www.isbc.com) site is a treasure trove of information for small business/SOHO entities, with such things as discussion groups, networking, and links to other domestic and international businesses, and business issues and newsletters.

- My Shopping Online (www.myshoppingonline.com) features legal do-it-yourself legal kits for a variety of things, many of them business related.
- Online Women's Business Center (www.onlinewbc.gov) is the SBA's online women's business center site devoted to female entrepreneurs.
- Small Business Advisor (www.isquare.com). This omnibus site provides small business information and advice, links to other sites, and contains numerous resources such as access to newsletters, reports, and government business and tax information/services.
- Smartbiz (www.smartbiz.com) is a site devoted to providing lists and links to free resources for small businesses such as publications, catalogs, and information.
- Verizon SuperPages (www.superpages.com) is a directory assistance Yellow Pages for the Internet and costs $25.00 per month to get your business listed in it. This might bring in business and is relatively inexpensive.
- Vfinance.com (www.vfinance.com) is a site that provides information and links to venture capital/angel investor resources for the entrepreneur.

Media

- CNBC, MSNBC, Fox News Channel, and CNN. These networks provides a host of business shows, many with small business topics at various times in the day. Especially useful is CNBC's morning line-up and its approach of following the stock market all day. Since the times and the shows have a tendency to change often on cable, check local listings or visit the network websites for further information.
- Local Broadcasting. Many network television affiliates and local PBS stations have business shows, especially during the noon hour or noon news. These might be sources of information or ways to promote your business (as a guest). Most talk radio stations have local programs, many business related. Check your local dials.
- Nightly Business Report on PBS. This program provides an overview of the day's business and financial news. Some of it directly pertains to small businesses.

Organizations and Groups

- American Association of Franchisees & Dealers. This group is a franchise organization that provides information, benefits, publication, and assistance to potential franchisees. Call 1-800-733-9858, visit their website at www.aafd.org, or write:

  AAFD
  P.O. Box 81887
  San Diego, CA 92138-1887

- American Success Institute. The ASI helps people starting businesses through a collection of resources and publications devoted to small and growing businesses. For more information, check out its website at www.success.org, phone 1-800-585-1300, or write:

  ASI
  5 N. Main Street
  Nantick, MA 01760

- Better Business Bureau. These bureaus are in all cities across the nation. The purpose is self-regulation and grievance redress. By joining, you receive the satisfaction that the BBB on your front counter brings. Call your local BBB for information on joining. It also has an online program. Check out the national BBB website www.bbbonline.org.

- Chamber of Commerce. Most Chambers are made up of small businesses just like you. That's the backbone. Chambers provide members with information and networking and business opportunities. The Chamber will work for your local business area. Membership is a good idea.

- Direct Marketing Association. This is a mail-order association that you can join if you plan mail-order sales. It provides services and information that may be of value or use. Check out the website at www.thedma.org, or write:

  DMA
  1120 Avenue of the Americas
  New York, NY 10036

- Entrepreneur Media, Inc. This company is dedicated to providing information and assistance for small businesses and entrepreneurs. It publishes *Entrepreneur* magazine (see "Periodic Publications"). For information, call (949) 261-2325, visit the website at www.entrepreneur.com, or write:

Entrepreneur Media
2445 McCabe Way
Irvine, CA 92614

- International Franchise Association. This is similar to the AAFD and will provide information, booklets, and benefits to members. It puts out a publication called Franchise World. A good place to start your franchise research. Call (202) 628-8000, visit their website at www.franchise.org, or write:

  IFA
  1350 New York Ave, NW Suite 900
  Washington, DC 20005-4709

- Liberty Tree. A group that puts out a catalog with libertarian and free market publications. Many relate to small businesses. For more information, visit www.liberty-tree.org.

- National Association for the Self-Employed. This group publishes two magazines for small business owners, including Self-Employed America, and provides information and benefits for members who are usually small business owners. Visit www.nase.org or write:

  NASE
  P.O. Box 612067
  DWF Airport
  Dallas, TX 75261-2067

- National Association of Women Business Owners. This group lobbies for women's businesses and has information and services. Visit the website at www.nawbo.org or write:

  National Association of Women Business Owners
  1595 Spring Hill Rd
  Suite 330
  Vienna, VA 22182

- National Federation of Independent Businesses. This group of 600,000 businesses is a lobbying organization for small businesses. It is one of the most powerful small business organizations in the nation. Call them at (615) 872-5800 or 1-800-NFIB-NOW, visit their website at www.nfibonline.com, or write to:
  NFIB

1201 F Street NW
Suite 200
Washington, DC 20004

- National Small Business United. This is an established business advocate for small businesses. The website is www.nsbu.org.
- The New Careers Center. This publisher produces a catalog with a variety of great small business publications. Here is a sample list of their titles:

    How to Form Your Own Corporation without a Lawyer
    Guerrilla Financing: Alternative Techniques to Finance Any Small Business
    Working Solo Sourcebook: Essential Resources for Independent
      Entrepreneurs
    Ecopreneuring
    The Work-At-Home Sourcebook
    The Complete Work-At-Home Companion
    Home Business 101
    Free Money from the Federal Government for Small Businesses
      and Entrepreneurs
    Small Time Operator
    The Start Up Guide: A One Year Plan for Entrepreneurs
    Starting and Operating a Business In . . . (each state has a guide)
    Marketing for the Home-Based Business
    The Complete Small Business Loan Kit

    This is just a sampling of the great books for small business owners. We recommend ordering their catalog.

    Write:
    New Careers Center
    1515 23rd Street
    Box 339-AT
    Boulder, CO 80306

- SOHO America Association. This group represents SOHO businesses as an organization and provides networking, news and stories, and benefits such as discount travel and health insurance. They also keep tabs on the state of SOHO businesses. SOHO encourages you to visit the website www.soho.org for information, or write:

    SOHO

P.O. Box 941
Hurst, TX 76053

Periodic Publications

- *Business Start-Ups*. This magazine presents ideas for new and potential entrepreneurs. It usually has four or five feature articles and has several departments with information and news relevant to all small businesses. Usually available at newsstands.
- *Entrepreneur*. This monthly focuses on starting and growing a business, with a hands-on approach focusing on current trends. Available at newsstands everywhere or from www.entrepreneur.com.
- *Fast Company*. A hip, fast-paced business magazine devoted to reporting on business news and trends, and on successful entrepreneurs and cutting-edge companies. This magazine is a trendy, off-beat publication that doesn't read stodgy like many established magazines. If you want a unique perspective on business, this is for you. Available at newsstands or www.enews.com.
- *Home Business Magazine*. A semi-monthly magazine on running a SOHO business. It contains articles and information on everything from business opportunities to the Internet to legal issues to selling and marketing. Available at newsstands or at amazon.com.
- *Home Business Rep*. Another magazine on SOHO business, this one geared at microbusinesses, providing tips, news, and advice on making these smallest of businesses successful. Published in Canada (with information applicable anywhere), it's available at www.enews.com.
- *INC*. This magazine is for somewhat larger companies and even corporations, but *INC* usually has a great deal of small business news and articles. It is available at newsstands.
- *Opportunity World*. This magazine reports on entrepreneurs with a focus on the success of individual firms, the methods to achieve success, and developing winning business ideas. Available at newsstands or at www.enews.com.
- *Wall Street Journal, Business Week, Fortune, Forbes, Barrons, Money, USA Today, Worth Magazine, The Economist*, and *Kiplingers*. These heavy hitters

cover the corporate and small business worlds. You should browse through them now and then to see if there is anything that might be of use to you. They are a great way to keep abreast of industry trends and the economy as a whole.

Services

- Business Training Media. This company has information on starting a variety of businesses, offering online and by-mail packages on everything from automotive businesses to self-publishing. Most were from the *Entrepreneur* line of how-to products, but they are offered here along with online, CD-ROM, and multimedia products. Visit www.businesstrainingmedia.com for more information, or write:
  Pacific Business Marketing
  4694 White Oak Avenue
  Encino, CA 91316
- CCH, Inc. (Business Owner's Toolkit). This company provides publications and information on everything from marketing to employees to business startups to aspiring small business owners. Its website at www.toolkit.cch.com is excellent; many free resources are located here. For more information, write:
  CCH, Inc
  2700 Lake Cook Rd
  Riverwoods, IL 60015
- Charles Schwab, ETRADE, DATEK, AMERITRADE. For personal finance, you might want to check out a discount online brokerage like these. You have control of your money and make your own investing decisions, enabling you to make the most of your personal finances, which could play a role in future business financing plans.
- The Company Corporation. This company will incorporate you or form your LLC for a fee in any of the states. Prices start at $49.00 plus filing fees. Call 1-800-818-0204 or visit the website at www.incorporate.com for more information. Write:
  Company Corporation
  2711 Centerville Road, Suite 400

Wilmington, DE 19808

- EDR Payment Services. This company offers credit card accepting/processing systems. Visit it at www.edronline.com or call-800-822-0988 for information.
- Kmart Supplier Diversity Department. This is a minority-diversity-based program by Kmart that enables a review of a minority-operated company's product for possible placement in Kmart stores. According to the website, it will still operate under the Kmart restructuring. Write:
  Kmart Supplier Diversity Department
  3100 West Big Beaver Road
  Troy, MI 48084
- Lab Safety Supply, Inc. has a catalog of safety supplies and has a listing of labor, environmental, food, and transportation regulation manuals. Visit www.labsafety.com or call 1-800-3560-0783 for a catalog.
- Merchant Bankcard Network. Visit www.mastercard-visa.com for information on credit card accepting systems, or call 1-800-207-2231.
- Merchant's Choice Card Services also offers information on credit card accepting systems. Call 1-800-687-2776 for information.
- National Business Library Start-Up Guides. These guides will help you start one of dozens of businesses. These blueprints contain a plethora of stats, strategies, and information for about forty dollars each. Call 1-800-947-7724 for more information.
- Pitney Bowes can help you with mailing and information systems. Check your local Yellow Pages.
- Staples Inc. is not just a supply store; Staples also provides business services, advice, and connections to other small businesses. Visit the website at www.staples.com or write:
  Staples
  4535 Rosewood Drive
  Pleasanton, CA 94588
- Uniform Code Council provides bar coding information and services to businesses.
  UCC, Inc
  P.O. Box 1244
  Dayton, OH 45401

Suppliers

- American Business Lists is a company that supplies mailing lists of nine million businesses and seventy-eight million individuals. Call (402) 331-7169 for information.
- American Business Resources, Inc. This company sells policy manuals, employee handbooks, and other products that might be useful for growing businesses. Visit the website at www.bizmanuals.com.
- Dome Publishing (www.domeind.com). This company publishes books on bookkeeping, payroll, budget books, and computer software. You can buy them at office supply stores, at www.buyonlinenow.com, or by writing:

  Dome Publishing
  10 New England Way
  Warwick, RI 02886

- NEBS, Inc. This company produces business forms for advertising, bidding, billing, check writing, documenting, labeling, mailing, organizing, and selling. Write to them for a catalog, although as a new business they may mail you one eventually anyway. Visit the website at www.nebs.com or call 1-800-225-6380.

  NEBS, Inc
  500 Main Street
  Groton, MA 01471

- Office Depot, Staples, Office Max, and Best Buy. These are national chain business and computer/software supply stores. They often beat local competitors on prices. The first three carry an array of supplies, books, computers, furniture, and office/stationery products. The later has a line of business software and computers.
- Reliable sells office equipment through mail order. Visit the website at www.reliable.com or write to them for a catalog:

  Reliable
  1001 Van Buren Street
  Chicago, IL 60607

- Software. The industry standard has become Windows-based programs. These include Word Perfect and Microsoft Word for word processing, Lotus and Excel for spreadsheets, and Money for finance management, as well as Quickbooks Pro or Peachtree Accounting for accounting and billing. Database programs include FoxPro and Access. All are available at software stores and chains.

- World's Easiest Software. This is available at many office supply or software stores. It has software to make business cards, certificates, promotional materials, and other essential business documents. Visit the website at www.easiestbiz.com for online shopping.

In addition, there are literally hundreds and thousands of suppliers of specific items for businesses as well as hundreds of industry-specific publications and service providers. To check for suppliers for equipment unique to your business, we suggest you consult the Yellow Pages of your phone book and those of larger cities such as Chicago, New York, Los Angeles, Detroit, Atlanta, Boston, San Francisco, and so on. Many industry magazines (those relating to your specific business) have excellent advertising sections where suppliers advertise their companies and products.

Another excellent place to obtain product/supplier information is trade shows. These are held all over the country and cover all businesses. Here, related suppliers, dealers, and manufacturers gather under one roof to display their products and services. You can obtain information directly from company representatives at the trade show or convention. Not only is it a good way to see products up close and in person, but it is a great way to make contacts inside the supplier company.

This list is by no means exhaustive. Many trade journals and academic journals can be consulted, as can colleges (business and economics professors), government publications and agencies, and private think tanks.

Chapter

State Requirements

▶ **Sample incorporation steps**

▶ **Sample letters to your state**

▶ **Business checklist worksheet**

▶ **State requirements**

This chapter lists state offices and addresses, statistics, and requirements. We have updated not only the start-up information for each state, but have also included more sources of help within each state. These sources include business investment centers, minority business development agencies, websites, and first-stop business locations. Not all states have the same amount or quality of sources, but each at least has a Small Business Development Center and a website.

The secretary of state generally handles incorporations; revenue handles state sales tax numbers, use numbers, tax, and exempt numbers. That office can send you the necessary forms and may answer some questions you have. Still, be sure to ask a lawyer, accountant, and/or one of the other sources listed above for thorough consultation. Utilizing the SBA and its resources is usually a good bet.

In our first two editions, we surveyed the secretaries of state and the revenue offices of all fifty states and the District of Columbia. They provided us with forms and information, and answered questionnaires we mailed. For this edition, we used the power of the Internet to update and streamline the state information, using each state website to update the 1997 information. That said, we feel it is important to remember that although our information is current, relying on outdated information can cause you to be fined for improper action by the state at worst, or have your filing information returned as incomplete at the least. Therefore, you should use this as a guide only, not as the definitive truth. Any misprints or deletions are unintentional, and if you use the information without first consulting a lawyer, contacting your state, or browsing the state website's current information, you do so at your own risk. Again, the facts are as complete as we could make them with the information supplied by state websites as of 2002. Any new state laws or regulations should be noted by you and your lawyer, and followed.

That said, most state requirements are very similar, following predictable patterns. Generally, you will need to secure a Federal Identification Number, register your business entity with your state and local officials, and obtain state tax registration. Along the way, you may have to apply for licenses or other permits as well, some at the local level. But that is all the actual start-up is generally composed of. Within each registration phase might be other phases.

If you are going to start a sole proprietorship or a general partnership, you generally just need to register with your county official, usually the clerk or recorder. Sometimes you will need a city business license as well. Call to find out. There may also be zoning restrictions or requirements to consider.

For corporations and limited liability companies, the process is more involved. Figure 13.1 contains a sample of the steps one might take to incorporate in Indiana.

Figure 13.1: SAMPLE INDIANA INCORPORATION STEPS

State Business Registration

- File an Application for Reservation of Corporate Name, Form 26233
- File the Articles of Incorporation, Form 5149

Local Business Registration

- Register with the county recorder

State Tax Registration

- File form BT-1 for withholding tax, sales and use tax and to get a tax-exempt ID number

Licenses

- While going through the process, obtain any and all licenses and permits you will need. A lawyer is a good person to talk to if you think you need these.

As you can see in this simplified example, just a few forms were filed. The total cost would be around $150, including any recording fees, but excluding any fees for a lawyer or an accountant. The process will take a few weeks, but you can always expedite things over the phone. Many states offer one- or two-day expedited services for higher fees. If you are in a hurry, this might be for you. State fees vary, and do not forget, you can form a corporation in states like Nevada or Delaware even if you do not live there.

Many states strongly suggest using a lawyer when you incorporate, but again, that is up to you. We also think it is a good idea to use a lawyer for all aspects of incorporation, especially when filing for foreign corporation, limited liability company/partnership, or limited partnership status in another state. This is merely to protect you from legal, tax, and regulatory problems. A foreign corporation, limited liability company, or limited partnership is an entity formed in another state under different laws (albeit very similar laws). Thus, if you are an Indiana corporation and set up a shop or do business in Ohio, you must register in Ohio as a foreign corporation. The regulations here can be tricky, so get legal help first. Note, too, that if your business plan calls for stores or transactions across state lines, plan your filing of requirements early so that when the time comes, you can register as a foreign corporation without delay. Also, foreign corporations are often asked to obtain certificates of existence or good standing from their original state when filing foreign corporation forms.

Most states also require that certain entities have "Company," "Corporation," "Incorporated," "Limited Liability Company," or "Limited Partnership" as part of the name (in most, the abbreviations of the words are suitable). Your state will send information on this, but it is a good idea to plan on using one of the words or an abbreviation.

Assumed or fictitious names are those used generally by partnerships or sole proprietors when their business name is different from their entity name. Sometimes companies use a Doing Business As (DBA) statement to use a name different from their actual name.

Other start-up considerations are annual reports for corporations, some partnerships, and limited liability companies; securities regulations for corporations; employment commissions and agencies; and regulatory boards and other requirements such as Uniform Commercial Code filings. This is where a lawyer or your state offices can provide more detailed information. This book is not designed to cover everything concerning every business or industry. Still, you do not want to get bogged down after you have started business because you did not file all of the proper papers with the proper agencies or do not have all the right permits.

In Figure 13.2 and 13.3 on the following pages, we have included two sample letters that you can use as guides for obtaining information from the secretary of state and/or the state revenue office. They are guides only, and your letters should be unique and in your own words. However, you want to state your purpose and what information/services you desire. Many states appreciate a self-addressed 9 X 12 envelope. Since you do not know how much the return mail will cost, omit postage.

Do, however, write the state for information beforehand. The information provided below is intended to guide you and open your mind to the complexity of starting a business. For further information on any of the aspects below, write to the applicable state. Also, visit the state website. Our research for this new edition showed that every state has a plethora of business start-up information, including forms, fees, and general information to assist you in the process. Many states also have created omnibus business sites focusing on start-up requirements, forms, and laws. These are meant to streamline information-gathering for the would-be businessperson by gathering a wide-ranging variety of state-specific information, websites, and requirements. Additionally, many states now have streamlined business filing programs utilizing the Internet. Again, check your state's website for the availability of such a program.

Following the letters is a Business Checklist Worksheet in Figure 13.4 to help you keep the process in order. Additionally, Appendix D contains a worksheet designed to help you research the start-up needs and requirements for your small business. Remember to use our information, as well as any you glean from the state sources listed below.

Figure 13.2: **LETTER ONE**

Date

Your Address

Secretary of State

Capitol Bldg

Capital City, Anystate 00000

To Whom It May Concern:

I am in the process of researching my small business start-up and would like any information you may have.

Could you please send me information on the following type of business entities: (Pick only those you need information on)

1. Sole Proprietors
2. Partnerships
3. Corporations
4. Limited Liability Company
5. Limited Liability Partnership

I need information relating to fees, procedures, regulations, and rules. In addition, any forms or publications your office has will be greatly appreciated.

Thank you for your time and consideration. I look forward to your reply.

Sincerely,

Your Name

Figure 13.3: **LETTER TWO**

Date

Your Address

Department of Revenue

A Street

Capital City, Anystate 00000

To Whom It May Concern:

Please send to me the proper forms and documentation to obtain a sales tax and/or use number, and for other applicable state taxes such as income withholding.

In addition, any additional tax information concerning small businesses in Anystate will be greatly appreciated. I intend to use this information with my lawyer and/or accountant while I go through the process of starting my business.

Thank you for your time and consideration. I look forward to your reply.

Sincerely,

Your Name

Figure 13.4: BUSINESS CHECKLIST WORKSHEET

Business Entity:

❑ Sole Proprietorship

❑ General Partnership

❑ Limited Partnership

❑ Limited Liability Company

❑ Limited Liability Partnership

❑ Corporation

❑ S Corporation

Checklist Steps:

❑ Federal EIN—Form SS-4: Federal Level

❑ Entity Name Reservation: State Level

Form(s):_____

❑ Tax Registration

Sales, Use, Withholding, Excise, Other:_____

Form(s):_____

Form(s):_____

❑ Business Registration: State Level

Form(s):_____

❑ Trade Name Registration: State Level

Form(s):_____

❑ Business Registration: Local/County Level

Licenses/Form(s):_____

❑ State/Local Licensing or Permits

Agency:_____

Phone Number:_____

Form(s):_____

Agency:_____

Phone Number:_____

Form(s):_____

❏ Workers Compensation Insurance/Other Employment Necessities

Agency:_____

Phone Number:_____

Form(s):_____

Agency:_____

Phone Number:_____

Form(s):_____

❏ Assumed or Fictitious Name Registration/Doing Business As Registration

Form(s):_____

❏ Trademark, Copyright, or Patent: Federal Level and Certain States (TM)

Type Needed (If any):_____

_____

_____

State Requirements

As a final reminder, remember that there may be other requirements you need to look into, or that some requirements may change as states enact new laws or overhaul old bureaucratic systems. Be sure, therefore, to write your state first and get all the facts. This way, you can be sure. And don't forget local regulations. Your lawyer can tell you about them, as can your county recorder, city clerk or county clerk, local incubator, city government, or Chamber of Commerce.

Alabama

Office of the Secretary of State
Attn: Corporate Section
Montgomery, AL 36103
(334) 242-1170

Department of Revenue
50 N. Ripley
P.O. Box 5616,
Montgomery, AL 36132
(334) 242-5324

Business Registration Requirements

Incorporation:
- Certificate of Name Reservation
- Articles of Incorporation

Limited Liability Company:
- Articles of Organization
- Report of Domestic LLC

Limited Liability Partnership:
- Domestic Registered Liability Partnership

Limited Partnership:
- File the Limited Liability Partnership Registration

Sole Proprietor and General Partnership:
- Check with your county recorder or local officials

Foreign Entities:
- Corporations, limited liability companies, limited partnerships, and other businesses must file forms to transact business in the state. The fees and forms vary. They can be obtained from the state's website or

write to the Secretary of State.

Tax Registration Requirements

Sales and Withholding Tax:
- Contact the Department of Revenue for current information on taxes

In-state Help and Information
- Alabama does not have a Business Information Center (BIC) as of 2002
- SBA Office, Birmingham. Phone (205) 290-7101
- Local Small Business Development Center locations can be obtained at www.sba.gov/sbdc
- Local SCORE locations can be obtained at www.score.org
- State website: www.state.al.us

Alaska

Dept of Comm. & Econ Dev
Division of Corporations
P.O. Box 110808
Juneau, AK 99811-0808
(907) 465-2530

Dept of Revenue
333 Willoughby Ave 11th Flr
P.O. Box 110420
Juneau, AK 99811-0400
(907) 465-2375

Business Registration Requirements

Incorporation:
- Application for Reservation of Name
- Articles of Incorporation
- Application for Registration of Name
- The Biennial Corporation Tax
- Statement of SIC code
- You may also need to file an Alaska Business License Application

Limited Liability Company:
- Application for Reservation of Name (might be optional)
- Articles of Organization
- Application for Registration of Name

- You may also need to file an Alaska Business License Application

Limited Liability Partnership:
- Application for Reservation of Name (might be optional)
- Articles of Organization
- Application for Registration of Name
- You may also need to file an Alaska Business License Application

Limited Partnership:
- Application for Reservation of Name (might be optional)
- Application for Registration of Name
- Certificate of Limited Partnership
- Alaska Business License Application

Sole Proprietor and General Partnership:
- Alaska Business License Application
- Check with local officials on other licenses or permits

Foreign Entities:
- Corporations, limited liability companies, limited partnerships, and other businesses must file forms to transact business in the state. The fees and forms vary. They can be obtained from the Secretary of State's address above.

Tax Registration Requirements

Sales and Withholding Tax:
- Alaska has no state sales tax, use tax, or personal income taxes. Some cities and local governments do have taxes, however. Check your city or borough.

In-state Help and Information
- Alaska does not have a Business Information Center (BIC) as of 2002
- SBA Office: Anchorage, Phone: (907) 271-4022
- Local Small Business Development Center locations can be obtained at www.sba.gov/sbdc.
- Local SCORE locations can be obtained at www.score.org.
- State website: www.state.ak.us

Arizona

Arizona Corporation Commission
1300 W. Washington
Phoenix, AZ 85007-2929
(602) 542-3135

Dept of Revenue
1600 W Monroe
Phoenix, AZ 85007-2650
(800) 843-7196

Business Registration Requirements

Incorporation:
- Reserve a name with the Arizona Corporation Commission
- Articles of Incorporation
- Certificate of Disclosure
- Affidavit of Publication

Limited Liability Company:
- Articles of Organization
- Affidavit of Publication

Limited Partnership:
- Reserve a name with the Arizona Corporation Commission
- Certificate of Limited Partnership

Sole Proprietor and General Partnership:
- Check with your local and county governments for licensing information

Foreign Entities:
- Corporations, limited liability companies, limited partnerships, and other businesses must file forms to transact business in the state. The fees and forms vary. They can be obtained from the Secretary of State's address above.

Tax Registration Requirements

Transaction Privilege Tax and Withholding:
- Arizona Joint Tax Application, which also registers you for other taxes

In-state Help and Information
- Arizona does not have a Business Information Center (BIC) as of 2002. SBA Office: Phoenix, Phone: (602) 745-7200
- Local Small Business Development Center locations can be obtained at www.sba.gov/sbdc

- Local SCORE locations can be obtained at www.score.org
- State website: www.state.az.gov

Arkansas

Secretary of State
Off of the Sect of State
State Capitol Rm 256
Little Rock, AR 72201-1094
(501) 682-1010

Revenue Division
Dept of Finance & Admin
P.O. Box 1272
Rock, AR 72203
(501) 682-7104

Business Registration Requirements

Incorporation:
- Application for Reservation of Corporate Name
- Articles of Incorporation
- Franchise Tax Registration
- S Corporations must file an Arkansas AR-1103 form

Limited Liability Company:
- Application for Reservation of Limited Liability Company Name
- Articles of Organization

Limited Liability Partnership:
- Application for Qualification of Limited Liability Partnership

Limited Liability Limited Partnership:
- Application for Registration of Limited Liability Limited Partnership

Limited Partnership:
- Certificate of Limited Partnership

General Partnership:
- Statement of Partnership Authority

Sole Proprietor
- Check your county recorder and local agencies for requirements

Foreign Entities:
- Corporations, limited liability companies, limited partnerships, and other businesses must file forms to transact business in the state. The fees and forms vary. They can be obtained from the Secretary of State's address above.

Tax Registration Requirements

Sales Tax:
- Application for Permit to register for the sales tax permit

Withholding Tax:
- Withholding Registration

In-state Help and Information
- Business Information Center at Arkansas State University: Phone: (870) 910-8063
- SBA Office: Little Rock. Phone: (501) 324-5871
- Local Small Business Development Center locations can be obtained at www.sba.gov/sbdc
- Local SCORE locations can be obtained at www.score.org
- State website: www.state.ar.us

California

Secretary of State
1500 11th Street
Sacramento, CA 95814
(916) 653-6814

State Board of Equalization
P.O. Box 942879
Sacramento, CA 94279-0090
(800) 400-7115

Business Registration Requirements

Incorporation:
- Certificate of Reservation of Corporate Name
- Articles of Incorporation

Limited Liability Company:
- Certificate of Reservation of Limited Liability Company Name
- Articles of Organization
- Initial Statement of Information

Limited Liability Partnership:
- Registration of Limited Liability Partnership

Limited Partnership:
- Certificate of Reservation of Limited Partnership Name

- Certificate of Limited Partnership

General Partnership:
- Statement of Partnership Authority
- Check with the county recorder's and local government for further regulations

Sole Proprietor:
- Check with the county recorder's and local government for further regulations

Foreign Entities:
- Corporations, limited liability companies, limited partnerships, and other businesses must file forms to transact business in the state. The fees and forms vary. They can be obtained from the Secretary of State's address above.

Tax Registration Requirements

Sales Tax:
- You must obtain a sellers permit (for each business location) from your local Equalization Board. Write or check the website for a list of local Boards. The forms are Corporation/LLC: BOE-400-MCO or Partnership/sole proprietor: BOE-400-MIP.

Withholding Tax:
- File as a new employer

In-state Help and Information

- The Business Information Centers (BICs) are in Chula Vista, Phone: (619) 482-6393; Los Angeles, Phone: (213) 251-7253; San Diego, Phone: (619) 557-7250
- California has six SBA district offices: Fresno: (559) 487-5791, Glendale: (818) 552-3210, Sacramento: (916) 498-6410, San Diego: (619) 557-7250, San Francisco: (415) 744-6820, and Santa Ana: (714) 550-7420
- Local Small Business Development Center locations can be obtained at www.sba.gov/sbdc
- Local SCORE locations can be obtained at www.score.org
- State website: www.state.ca.us or www.boe.ca.gov for the Board of Equalization

Colorado

Secretary of State
Department of State
1560 Broadway, Suite 200
Denver, CO 80202 (303) 238-7378

Dept of Revenue
1375 Sherman St
Denver, CO 80261
(303) 894-2251

Business Registration Requirements

Incorporation:
- Reserve and register a name
- Articles of Incorporation

Limited Liability Company:
- Reserve a name
- Articles of Organization

Limited Liability Partnership:
- Limited Liability Partnership form (Also there are two other types of entity, which would file either Limited Liability Limited Partnership form or Limited Partnership Association form.)

Limited Partnership:
- Certificate of Limited Partnership

Sole Proprietor and General Partnership:
- Check with your county recorder and city officials for their regulations

Foreign Entities:
- Corporations, limited liability companies, limited partnerships and other businesses must file forms to transact business in the state. The fees and forms vary. They can be obtained from the Secretary of State's address above.

Tax Registration Requirements

Sales and Withholding Tax:
- Colorado Business Registration form, CR-100

In-state Help and Information

- The Business Information Center (BIC) is in Denver, Phone: (303) 844-2607

- SBA Office: Denver, Phone: (303) 844-2607
- Local Small Business Development Center locations can be obtained at www.sba.gov/sbdc
- Local SCORE locations can be obtained at www.score.org
- State website: www.state.co.us

Connecticut

Secretary of State
30 Trinity Street
Hartford, CT 06106
(806) 509-6212
In State (806) 566-7120

Dept of Revenue Services
25 Sigourney Street
Hartford, CT 06106
(800) 382-9463

Business Registration Requirements

Incorporation:
- Application for Reservation of Corporate Name
- Certificate of Incorporation & Organization and First Report
- State has both stock and non-stock corporations, and the requirements are similar, through the forms vary.

Limited Liability Company:
- Application for Reservation of Name
- Articles of Organization including Appointment of Statutory Agent

Limited Liability Partnership:
- Application to Reserve a Limited Liability Partnership Name
- Certificate of Limited Liability Partnership

Limited Partnership:
- Application for Reservation of Limited Partnership Name
- Certificate of Limited Partnership and Appointment of Statutory Agent

Sole Proprietor and General Partnership:
- Check your county recorder or town clerk

Foreign Entities:
- Corporations, limited liability companies, limited partnerships, and other businesses must file forms to transact business in the state. The

fees and forms vary. They can be obtained from the Secretary of State's address above.

Tax Registration Requirements

Sales and Withholding Tax:

- Business Taxes Registration Application REG-1

In-state Help and Information

- The Business Information Center (BIC) is in Hartford, Phone: (860) 251-7000
- SBA Office: Hartford, Phone: (860) 240-4700
- Local Small Business Development Center locations can be obtained at www.sba.gov/sbdc
- Local SCORE locations can be obtained at www.score.org
- State website: www.state.ct.us

Delaware

Secretary of State
401 Federal Street
Suite 3
Dover, DE 19901
(302) 739-3073

Division of Revenue
Dept of Finance
820 N French St
Wilmington, DE 19801
(302) 577-8200

Business Registration Requirements

Incorporation:

- The state suggests you contact a registered agent prior to starting the process. The state website has a list of such agents. The agent must have an address in Delaware.
- Reserve a name by telephone (corporations only): 1-900-420-8042
- Stock Certificate of Incorporation, Non-Stock Certificate of Incorporation, or Close Corporation Certificate of Incorporation

Limited Liability Company:

- Name Reservation Application

- Limited Liability Company Formation

Business Trusts:
- Name Reservation Application
- Business Trust Certificate

Limited Liability Partnership:
- Name Reservation Application
- Limited Liability Partnership Statement of Qualification

Limited Partnership:
- Name Reservation Application
- Limited Partnership Certificate

Sole Proprietor and General Partnership:
- Check the county recorder or clerk

Foreign Entities:
- Corporations, limited liability companies, limited partnerships, and other businesses must file forms to transact business in the state. The fees and forms vary. They can be obtained from the Secretary of State's address above.

Tax Registration Requirements
Sales and Withholding Tax:
- Combined Registration Application for withholding and other taxes; state has no sales tax.

In-state Help and Information
- The Business Information Center (BIC) is in Wilmington, Phone: (302) 831-1555
- SBA Office: Wilmington, Phone: (302) 573-2694
- Local Small Business Development Center locations can be obtained at www.sba.gov/sbdc
- Local SCORE locations can be obtained at www.score.org.
- State website: www.state.de.us

District of Columbia

Corporations Division
Dept of Consumer & Regulatory Aff.
941 N Capitol St, NE
Washington, DC 20002
(202) 442-4430

Office of Tax & Revenue
Customer Serv. Ctr., 1st Fl
941 N Capitol St, NE
Washington, DC 20002
(202) 727-4TAX

Business Registration Requirements

Incorporation:
- Application for Reservation of Corporate Name
- Articles of Incorporation

Limited Liability Company:
- Application for Reservation of Corporate Name
- Articles of Organization

Limited Liability Partnership:
- Application for Reservation of LLP Name
- Statement of Qualification of Limited Liability Partnership

Limited Partnership:
- Application for Reservation of Corporate Name
- Certificate of Limited Partnership
- Affirmation of Business Operation

Sole Proprietor and General Partnership:
- Register your business trade name
- GP's need a Statement of Partnership Authority
- You may need a Clean Hands Certificate or a Master Business License.

Foreign Entities:
- Corporations, limited liability companies, limited partnerships, and other businesses must file forms to transact business in the state. The fees and forms vary. They can be obtained from the Secretary of State's address above.

Tax Registration Requirements

Sales and Withholding Tax:
- Combined Registration Application for a variety of taxes

In-District Help and Information
- The Business Information Center (BIC), Phone: (202) 606-4000, ext. 266
- The SBA Field Office, Phone: (202) 606-4000
- Local Small Business Development Center locations can be obtained at www.sba.gov/sbdc
- Local SCORE locations can be obtained at www.score.org.
- State website: www.dc.gov

Florida

Department of State
Division of Corporations
P.O. Box 6327
Tallahassee, FL 32314
(850) 488-9000

Department of Revenue
5050 W. Tennessee Street
Tallahassee, FL 32399-0100
(800) 352-3671 (in FL only)

Business Registration Requirements

Incorporation:
- Reserve a name for 120 days
- Articles of Incorporation
- Certificate of Designation of Registered Agent/Registered Office

Limited Liability Company:
- Reserve a name for 120 days
- Articles of Organization

Limited Liability Partnership:
- Reserve a name for 120 days
- Partnership Registration Statement
- Statement of Qualification of Limited Liability Partnership

Limited Partnership:
- Reserve a name for 120 days
- Statement of Partnership Qualification (LLLP)
- Certificate of Limited Partnership
- Supplemental Affidavit (Capital Contributions)

General Partnership:

- Partnership Registration Statement
- Statement of Qualifications (For certain Partnerships)

Sole Proprietor:
- Check with your local and county governments

Foreign Entities:
- Corporations, limited liability companies, limited partnerships, and other businesses must file forms to transact business in the state. The fees and forms vary. They can be obtained from the Secretary of State's address above.

Tax Registration Requirements

Sales Tax:
- Application to Collect Tax in Florida (Form DR-1)

In-state Help and Information

- The Business Information Centers (BIC): Miami, Phone: 536-5521; Jacksonville, Phone: (904) 924-1100
- The SBA Field Offices are in Miami, Phone: (305) 536-5521 and Jacksonville, Phone: (904) 443-1900
- Local Small Business Development Center locations can be obtained at www.sba.gov/sbdc
- Local SCORE locations can be obtained at www.score.org
- State website: www.state.fl.us

Georgia

Secretary of State
Corporations Division
Suite 315, West Tower
2 Martin Luther King Jr., Dr.
Atlanta, GA 30334-1530
(404) 657-2817

Department of Revenue
Centralized Taxpayer
Registration Unit
P.O. Box 49512
Atlanta, GA 30359-1512
(404) 417-4490

Business Registration Requirements

Incorporation:
- Reserve a name
- Articles of Incorporation
- Transmittal Information Form
- Name Registration, Corporate Officers, & Annual Registration

Limited Liability Company:
- Reserve a name
- Articles of Organization
- Transmittal Information Form
- Name Registration

Limited Liability Partnership:
- Contact the state

Limited Partnership:
- Reserve a name
- Certificate of Limited Partnership
- Transmittal Information Form
- Name Registration

Sole Proprietor and General Partnership:
- Check with the county recorder or local offices

Foreign Entities:
- Corporations, limited liability companies, limited partnerships, and other businesses must file forms to transact business in the state. The fees and forms vary. They can be obtained from the Secretary of State's address above.

Tax Registration Requirements

Sales and Withholding Tax:
- State Tax Registration Application (CRF-002)

In-state Help and Information

- The Business Information Center (BIC) is in Atlanta, Phone: (404) 331-0100
- The SBA Field Office is in Atlanta, Phone: (404) 331-0100
- Local Small Business Development Center locations can be obtained at

www.sba.gov/sbdc
- Local SCORE locations can be obtained at www.score.org
- State website: www.state.ga.us

Hawaii

Dept of Commerce & Consumer Affairs
Business Registration
P.O. Box 40
Honolulu, HI 96810
(808) 586-2727

Dept of Taxation
P.O. Box 259
Honolulu, HI 96809-0259
(808) 587-4242

Business Registration Requirements

Incorporation:
- Application for Reservation of Name
- Articles of Incorporation (DC-1)
- Reserve Trade Name

Limited Liability Company:
- Application for Reservation of Name
- Articles of Organization for LLC (LLC-1)

Limited Liability Partnership:
- Application for Reservation of Name
- Certificate of LLP (LLP-1)

Limited Partnership:
- Application for Reservation of Name
- Certificate of Limited Partnership (LP-1)

General Partnership:
- Application for Reservation of Name
- Registration Statement for Partnership (GP-1)

Sole Proprietor:
- Check with the county recorder or local offices.

Foreign Entities:
- Corporations, limited liability companies, limited partnerships, and other businesses must file forms to transact business in the state. The

fees and forms vary. They can be obtained from the Secretary of State's address above.

Tax Registration Requirements

General Excise and Withholding Tax:
- Basic Business Application (BB-1), which registers you for a variety of taxes. Hawaii has a general excise tax, which is levied against the business.

In-state Help and Information
- The Business Information Center (BIC) is in Honolulu and the phone number is (808) 522-8130
- The SBA Field Office is in Honolulu, Phone: (808) 541-2990
- Local Small Business Development Center locations can be obtained at www.sba.gov/sbdc
- Local SCORE locations can be obtained at www.score.org
- State website: www.state.hi.us

Idaho

Secretary of State
P.O. Box 83720
Boise, ID 83720-0080
(208) 334-2300

State Tax Commission
800 Park, Plaza IV
Boise, ID 83722
(208) 334-7660
1-800-92-7660

Business Registration Requirements

Incorporation:
- Application for Reservation of Legal Entity Name
- Articles of Incorporation
- Application for Registration of Corporate Name

Limited Liability Company:
- Application for Reservation of Legal Entity Name
- Articles of Organization

Limited Liability Partnerships:

- Statement of Qualification of Limited Liability Partnership

Limited Partnership:

- Certificate of Limited Partnership

General Partnership:

- Statement of Partnership Authority

Sole Proprietor:

- Nothing needs to be done at the state level, but you might want to check county or local requirements.
- If needed, file the Certificate of Assumed Business Name.

Foreign Entities:

- Corporations, limited liability companies, limited partnerships, and other businesses must file forms to transact business in Indiana. The fees and forms vary. They can be obtained from the Secretary of State's address above.

Tax Registration Requirements

Sales and Withholding Tax:

- File form IBR-1, Idaho Business Registration Form, which will register you for sales, use, and withholding (among others) taxes.

In-state Help and Information

- The Business Information Center is in Boise, Phone: (208) 334-1696
- The SBA Field Office is in Boise, Phone: (208) 334-1696
- Local Small Business Development Center locations can be obtained at www.sba.gov/sbdc
- Local SCORE locations can be obtained at www.score.org
- State website: www.idoc.state.id.us

Illinois

Secretary of State
501 S. Second St, Suite 328
Springfield, IL 62756
(217) 782-6961

Dept of Revenue
101 W. Jefferson St
Springfield, IL 62702
(217) 524-4472

Business Registration Requirements

Incorporation:
- Reservation of Name, form BCA-4.10
- BCA-2.10 Articles of Incorporation
- Registration of Name, form BCA-4.25

Limited Liability Company:
- Reservation of Name, form LLC-1.15
- Articles of Organization, form LLC-5.5
- Application For Registration of Name, form LLC-45.20

Registered Limited Liability Partnership:
- Application for Registration of Limited Liability Partnership

Limited Partnership:
- Registration of Registered Agent, form LP-103c
- Certificate of Limited Partnership, form LP-201

Sole Proprietor and General Partnership:
- Nothing needs to be done at the state level; check your county and city officials.

Foreign Entities:
- Corporations, limited liability companies, limited partnerships, and other businesses must file forms to transact business in the state. The fees and forms vary. They can be obtained from the Secretary of State's address above.

Tax Registration Requirements

Sales and Withholding Tax:
- File the NUC-1 Illinois Business Registration. This will register you for sales tax, income, and withholding taxes among others. There may also be additional local taxes.

In-state Help and Information

- The Business Information Center (BIC) is in Chicago, Phone: (312) 886-0710
- The SBA Field Offices are in Chicago, Phone: (312) 353-4528; and Springfield, Phone: (217) 492-4416
- Local Small Business Development Center locations can be obtained at

www.sba.gov/sbdc
- Local SCORE locations can be obtained at www.score.org
- State website: www.state.il.us

Indiana

Secretary of State
State Capitol
Indianapolis, IN 46204
(317) 232-6531

Dept of Revenue
100 N Senate Ave
Indianapolis, IN 46204
(317) 233-4018

Business Registration Requirements

Incorporation:
- Application for Reserved Name
- Articles of Incorporation (State Form 4159)

Limited Liability Company:
- Application for Reserved Name
- File Articles of Organization

Limited Liability Partnership:
- Application for Reserved Name
- Limited Liability Partnership Registration

Limited Partnership:
- Application for Reserved Name
- Certificate of Limited Partnership

General Partnership and Sole Proprietor:
- Nothing needs to be done at the state level; filed at the County Recorder.

Foreign Entities:
- Corporations, limited liability companies, limited partnerships, and other businesses must file forms to transact business in the state. The fees and forms vary. They can be obtained from the Secretary of State's address above.

Tax Registration Requirements

Sales and Withholding Tax:

- All taxes including sales, withholding, corporate, use, and excise taxes are registered on form BT-1, Indiana Dept of Revenue Business Tax Application.

In-state Help and Information

- Indiana does not have a Business Information Center (BIC) as of 2002
- The SBA Field Office is in Indianapolis, Phone: (317) 226-7272
- Local Small Business Development Center locations can be obtained at www.sba.gov/sbdc
- Local SCORE locations can be obtained at www.score.org
- State website: www.state.in.us

Iowa

Secretary of State
Lucas Bldg, 1st Floor
E 12th Street
Des Moines, IA 50319
(515) 281-5864

Dept of Revenue & Finance
Hoover State Office Bldg
Des Moines, IA 50319
(515) 281-3204

Business Registration Requirements

Incorporation:

- Application to Reserve Corporate Name
- Articles of Incorporation

Limited Liability Company:

- Articles of Organization

Limited Liability Partnership:

- Statement of Qualifications for LLP

Limited Partnership:

- Application to Reserve Name
- Application for Certificate of Registration of Limited Partnership

Sole Proprietor and General Partnership:

- Nothing needs to be done at the state level. See the county recorder or your city officials for licensing information.

Foreign Entities:

- Corporations, limited liability companies, limited partnerships, and other businesses must file forms to transact business in the state. The fees and forms vary. They can be obtained from the Secretary of State's address above.

Tax Registration Requirements

Sales and Withholding Tax:

- Iowa Business Tax Registration (for a variety of taxes)

In-state Help and Information

- The Business Information Center (BIC), Waterloo, Phone: (319) 236-8123
- The SBA Field Offices are in Cedar Rapids, Phone: (319) 362-6405; and Des Moines, Phone: (515) 284-4422
- Local Small Business Development Center locations can be obtained at www.sba.gov/sbdc
- Local SCORE locations can be obtained at www.score.org
- State website: www.state.ia.us

Kansas

Secretary of State
120 SW 10th Ave
Topeka, KS 66612-1594
(785) 296-4564

Department of Revenue
915 SW Harrison St
Topeka, KS 66625
(785) 368-8222

Business Registration Requirements

Incorporation:

- Reservation of Corporate Name Form NR
- For Profit Articles of Incorporation Form CF

Limited Liability Company:

- Limited Liability Company Articles of Organization Form DL

Limited Liability Partnership:
- Limited Liability Partnership Statement of Qualification Form QLLP

Limited Partnership:
- Certificate of Limited Partnership Form CK

Sole Proprietor and General Partnership:
- Contact your county recorder or clerk and your local government for licensing or permits.

Foreign Entities:
- Corporations, limited liability companies, limited partnerships, and other businesses must file forms to transact business in the state. The fees and forms vary. They can be obtained from the Secretary of State's address above.

Tax Registration Requirements

Sales and Withholding Tax:
- CR-16, Business Tax Application. This will register you for a variety of taxes including sales and withholding.

In-state Help and Information
- Kansas does not have a Business Information Center (BIC) as of 2002
- The SBA Field Office is in Wichita, Phone: (316) 269-6616
- Local Small Business Development Center locations can be obtained at www.sba.gov/sbdc
- Local SCORE locations can be obtained at www.score.org
- First Stop Clearing House, Topeka. Phone: (913) 296-5298 (State suggests you call this for information on starting a business)
- State website: www.accesskansas.org

Kentucky

Secretary of State
Capitol Bldg Rm 152
Frankfort, KY 40601

Revenue Cabinet
200 Fair Oaks Lane
Frankfort, KY 40602

(502) 564-2849   (502) 564-4581

Business Registration Requirements

Incorporation:
- Application for Reserved Name
- Articles of Incorporation

Limited Liability Company:
- Application for Reserved Name
- Articles of Organization

Limited Liability Partnership:
- Statement of Registration of LLP

Limited Partnership:
- Application of Reservation of Name
- Certificate of Limited Partnership

General Partnership:
- If you are using an assumed name, file with the county clerk and the Secretary of State.

Sole Proprietor:
- Filed strictly in the county clerk's office and only if you are using an assumed name. Call for clarification as local information can change.

Foreign Entities:
- Corporations, limited liability companies, limited partnerships, and other businesses must file forms to transact business in the state. The fees and forms vary. They can be obtained from the Secretary of State's address above.

Tax Registration Requirements

Sales and Withholding Tax:
- Kentucky Tax Registration Application, Form 10A100

In-state Help and Information

- The Business Information Center (BIC), Louisville, Phone: (502) 574-1143
- The SBA Field Office is in Louisville, Phone: (502) 582-5761
- Local Small Business Development Center locations can be obtained at

www.sba.gov/sbdc
- Local SCORE locations can be obtained at www.score.org
- State website: www.kydirect.net

Louisiana

Secretary of State
Commercial Division
P.O. Box 94125
Baton Rouge, LA 70804-9125
(225) 925-4704

Dept of Revenue
P.O. Box 201
Baton Rouge, LA 70821-0201
(225) 219-7318

Business Registration Requirements

Incorporation:
- Name Reservation, Form #398
- Articles of Incorporation, Form #399
- Initial Report-Louisiana Business, Form #341

Limited Liability Company:
- Name Reservation, Form #398
- Articles of Organization, Form #365
- Limited liability Company Initial Report, Form #973

Limited Liability Partnership:
- Limited Liability Partnership-Registration, Form #975

Limited Partnership:
- Partnership Registration, Form #342
- Register with the recorder of mortgages in your parish of principal place of business.

General Partnership:
- The state made no distinction between limited and general partnerships, so check first with the state or your lawyer. As always check local and parish government.

Sole Proprietor:
- Filed with Clerk of Court in parish of domicile

Foreign Entities:

- Corporations, limited liability companies, limited partnerships, and other businesses must file forms to transact business in the state. The fees and forms vary. They can be obtained from the Secretary of State's address above.

Tax Registration Requirements
Sales Tax and Withholding Tax:
- Central Registration Application

In-state Help and Information
- Louisiana does not have a Business Information Center (BIC) as of 2002.
- The SBA Field Office is in New Orleans, Phone: (504) 589-6685
- Local Small Business Development Center locations can be obtained at www.sba.gov/sbdc
- Local SCORE locations can be obtained at www.score.org
- State website: www.state.la.us

Maine

Secretary of State
Division of Corporations
101State House Station
Augusta, ME 04333-101
(207) 624-7752

Revenue Services
24 State House Station
Augusta, ME 04333-0024
(207) 287-2076

Business Registration Requirements
Incorporation:
- Application for Reservation of Name, MBCA 1
- Articles of Incorporation, MBCA-6
- Application for Registration of Name, MBCA 2

Limited Liability Company:
- Application for Reservation of Name, MLLC 1
- Articles of Organization, MLLC 6

- Application for Registration of Name, MLLC 2

Limited Liability Partnership:
- Application for Reservation of Name, MLLP 1
- Certificate of Limited Liability Partnership, MLLP 6
- Application for Registration of Name, MLLP 2

Limited Partnership:
- Application for Reservation of Name, MLPA 1
- Certificate of Limited Partnership, MLPA 6
- Application for Registration of Name, MLPA 2

Sole Proprietor and General Partnership:
- Nothing needs to be done at the state level, check with your municipal clerk or county officials to file your business.

Foreign Entities:
- Corporations, limited liability companies, limited partnerships, and other businesses must file forms to transact business in the state. The fees and forms vary. They can be obtained from the Secretary of State's address above.

Tax Registration Requirements

Sales and Withholding Tax:
- Application for Tax Registration, which will also register you for other taxes

In-state Help and Information

- The Business Information Centers (BIC) are in Lewiston, Phone: (207) 782-3708, and Portland, Phone: (207)756-8180
- The SBA Field Office is in Augusta, Phone: (207) 622-8274
- Local Small Business Development Center locations can be obtained at www.sba.gov/sbdc
- Local SCORE locations can be obtained at www.score.org
- State website: www.state.me.us

Maryland

Dept of Assessments & Taxation
310 W Preston, Room 809
Baltimore, MD 21201
(410) 767-1184

Comptroller of Treasury
Revenue Administration Ctr
Annapolis, MD 21411-0001
(301) 225-1313

Business Registration Requirements

Incorporation:

- Register a corporate name with the state
- Articles of Incorporation for a Stock Corporation
- Or, Articles of Incorporation for a Nonstock Corporation
- Or, Articles of Incorporation for a Close Corporation

Limited Liability Company:

- Register a LLC name with the state
- Articles of Organization

Limited Liability Partnership:

- Register a LLP name with the state
- Certificate of Limited Liability Partnership

Limited Partnership:

- Register a LP name with the state
- Certificate of Limited Partnership

Sole Proprietor and General Partnership:

- Nothing needs to be done at the state level; check your local or county government.

Foreign Entities:

- Corporations, limited liability companies, limited partnerships, and other businesses must file forms to transact business in the state. The fees and forms vary. They can be obtained from the Secretary of State's address above.

Tax Registration Requirements

Sales and Withholding Tax:

- Combined Registration Application, which registers you for a variety of taxes

In-state Help and Information

- The Business Information Center (BIC) is in Cumberland, Phone: (301) 722-9300
- The SBA Field Office is in Baltimore, Phone: (410) 962-4392
- Local Small Business Development Center locations can be obtained at www.sba.gov/sbdc
- Local SCORE locations can be obtained at www.score.org
- State website: www.state.md.us

Massachusetts

Secretary of the Commonwealth
Corporations Division
One Ashburton Place, 17th Floor
Boston, MA 02108
(617) 727-9640

Dept of Revenue
P.O. Box 7011
Boston, MA 02204
(617) 887-6367

Business Registration Requirements

Incorporation:
- Reserve a name
- Articles of Organization

Limited Liability Company:
- You may want to reserve a name; the state was unclear on this.
- Certificate of Registration (No form, just registration)

Limited Liability Partnership:
- You may want to reserve a name; the state was unclear on this.
- File for registration with the Secretary of the Commonwealth

Limited Partnership:
- Reserve a name
- Certificate of Limited Partnership

General Partnership:
- DBA (Doing Business As) at the local city or town hall

Sole Proprietor:
- If it is under your name, you have no state requirements. If you are doing business with a different name than your own, file a DBA with

the local city or town hall.

Foreign Entities:

- Corporations, limited liability companies, limited partnerships, and other businesses must file forms to transact business in the state. The fees and forms vary. They can be obtained from the Secretary of State's address above.

Tax Registration Requirements

Sales and Withholding Tax:

- Form TA-1, Application for Original Registration, which is used for most tax registration
- Schedule TA-3 may be required as well

In-state Help and Information

- The Business Information Centers (BIC) are in Boston, Phone: (617) 565-5615; West Barnstable, Phone: (508) 362-2131; Pittsfield, Phone: (413) 448-2755; Fall River, Phone: (508) 673-9783; Lynn, Phone: (781) 477-7222; Worcester, Phone: (508) 363-0303; Brockton, Phone: (508) 586-0500; and Lawrence, Phone: (978) 686-2072
- The SBA Field Office is in Boston, Phone: (617) 565-5590
- Local Small Business Development Center locations can be obtained at www.sba.gov/sbdc
- Local SCORE locations can be obtained at www.score.org
- State website: www.state.ma.us

Michigan

Dept of Consumer & Industry Services
6546 Mercantile Way
Lansing, MI 48909
(517) 334-6206

Bureau of Revenue
Treasury Building
Lansing, MI 48909
(517) 373-0888

Business Registration Requirements

Incorporation:

- Application for Reservation of Name Form 540
- Articles of Incorporation Form 500 (Form 50 for Professionals)

Limited Liability Company:
- Reservation of Name Form 540
- Articles of Organization Form 700 (Form 701 for Professionals)

Limited Liability Partnership:
- Application to Register a Limited Liability Partnership

Limited Partnership:
- Certificate of Limited Partnership Form 401

Sole Proprietor and Copartnership:
- File at the county clerk for an assumed business name.
- For Copartnership, file a Certificate of Copartnership with the clerk.

Foreign Entities:
- Corporations, limited liability companies, limited partnerships, and other businesses must file forms to transact business in the state. They can be obtained from the Secretary of State's address above.

Tax Registration Requirements
Sales and Withholding Tax:
- Form 518, which registers you for a variety of taxes

In-state Help and Information
- The Business Information Centers (BICs) are in Flint, Phone: (810) 767-6455; and Grand Rapids, Phone: (616) 771-6880
- The SBA Field Office is in Detroit, Phone: (313) 226-6075
- Local Small Business Development Center locations can be obtained at www.sba.gov/sbdc
- Local SCORE locations can be obtained at www.score.org
- State website: www.michigan.gov

Minnesota

Secretary of State
180 State Office Bldg

Department of Revenue
Mail Station 4410

St. Paul, MN 55155   St. Paul, MN 55146-4410
(612) 296-2803   1-800-657-3605

Business Registration Requirements

Incorporation:
- Request for Reservation of Name
- Articles of Incorporation (or Articles of Incorporation for Cooperative for cooperatives)

Limited Liability Company
- Request for Reservation of Name
- Articles of Organization

Limited Liability Partnership:
- LLP Statement of Qualifications
- May need to file a Statement of Partnership Authority

Limited Partnership:
- LP Name Reservation
- Certificate of Limited Partnership
- May need to file a Statement of Partnership Authority

Sole Proprietor and General Partnership:
- Nothing needs to be done at the state level unless you need to file a Certificate of Assumed Name. Otherwise check your county and local officials for licensing and permits.

Foreign Entities:
- Corporations, limited liability companies, limited partnerships, and other businesses must file forms to transact business in the state. The fees and forms vary. They can be obtained from the Secretary of State's address above.

Tax Registration Requirements

Sales and Withholding Tax:
- Application for Business Registration, which registers you for a variety of taxes

In-state Help and Information
- The Business Information Center (BIC) is in Minneapolis, Phone: (612)

347-6747
- The SBA Field Office is in Minneapolis, Phone: (612) 370-2324
- Local Small Business Development Center locations can be obtained at www.sba.gov/sbdc
- Local SCORE locations can be obtained at www.score.org
- State website: www.state.mn.us

Mississippi

Secretary of State
P.O. Box 136
Jackson, MS 39205-1036
(601) 359-1350

State Tax Commission
P.O. Box 1033
Jackson, MS 39215-1033
(601) 923-7000

Business Registration Requirements

Incorporation:
- Reservation of Name
- Registration of Corporate Name
- Articles of Incorporation

Limited Liability Company:
- Application for Name Reservation
- Application for Appointment of Registered Agent (may be optional)
- Certificate of Formation

Limited Liability Partnership:
- Certificate of Registered Domestic LLP

Limited Partnership:
- Certificate of Mississippi Limited Partnership

Sole Proprietor and General Partnership:
- Nothing needs to be done at the state level; check your county and local governments

Foreign Entities:
- Corporations, limited liability companies, limited partnerships and other businesses must file forms to transact business in the state. The fees and forms vary. They can be obtained from the Secretary of State's

address above.

Tax Registration Requirements
Sales and Withholding Tax:
- File Registration Application, 70-001-00-1, which registers you for a variety of taxes

In-state Help and Information
- Mississippi does not have a Business Information Center (BIC) as of 2002.
- The SBA Field Offices are in Gulfport, Phone: (601) 863-4449; and Jackson, Phone: (601) 965-4378
- Local Small Business Development Center locations can be obtained at www.sba.gov/sbdc
- Local SCORE locations can be obtained at www.score.org
- State website: www.state.ms.us

Missouri

Secretary of State
Kirkpatrick State Information Ctr.
P.O. Box 778
Jefferson City, MO 65102
(573) 751-4153

Dept of Revenue
301 W High St
Room 330
Jefferson City, MO 65101
(573) 751-2836
1-800-877-6881 (forms only)

Business Registration Requirements
Incorporation:
- Application for Reservation of Name, LLC 3
- Articles of Incorporation, Corp 41
- Articles of Incorporation for a Close Corporation, Corp 41

Limited Liability Company:
- Application for Reservation of Name, LLC 3
- Articles of Organization, LLC 1

Limited Liability Partnership:
- Application for Reservation of Name, LLC 3
- Application for Registration of a Limited Liability Partnership, LLP 6

Limited Partnership:
- Application for Reservation of Name, LLC 3
- Certificate of Limited Partnership, LP 41

Limited Liability Limited Partnership:
- Application for Registration of a Missouri Limited Liability Limited Partnership, LP 24

Sole Proprietor and General Partnership:
- Nothing at state level unless you use a fictitious name; check your county government.

Foreign Entities:
- Corporations, limited liability companies, limited partnerships, and other businesses must file forms to transact business in the state. The fees and forms vary. In Missouri, though, some foreign corporations are allowed to do certain activities without registration. Check with the Secretary of State's office.

Tax Registration Requirements

Sales and Withholding Tax:
- Missouri Tax Registration Application, Form 2643, which will also register you for other taxes

In-state Help and Information

- The Business Information Center (BIC) is in Kansas City, Phone: (816) 374-6675
- The SBA Field Offices are in Kansas City, Phone: (816) 374-6708; and St. Louis, Phone: (314) 539-6600
- Local Small Business Development Center locations can be obtained at www.sba.gov/sbdc
- Local SCORE locations can be obtained at www.score.org
- State website: www.state.mo.us

Montana

Secretary of State
P.O. Box 202801
Helena, MT 59620-2801
(406) 444-3665

Department of Revenue
P.O. Box 5805
Helena, MT 59604-5805
(406) 444-6900

Business Registration Requirements

Incorporation:
- Application for Reservation of Name
- Articles of Incorporation

Limited Liability Company:
- Application for Reservation of Name
- Articles of Organization for Domestic Limited Liability Company

Limited Liability Partnership:
- Application for Reservation of Name
- Application for Registration of Limited Liability Partnership

Limited Partnership:
- Application for Reservation of Name
- Certificate of Limited Partnership

Sole Proprietor and General Partnership:
- Assumed Business Name if needed, otherwise see local authorities for licenses.

Foreign Entities:
- Corporations, limited liability companies, limited partnerships, and other businesses must file forms to transact business in the state. The fees and forms vary. They can be obtained from the Secretary of State's address above.

Tax Registration Requirements

Withholding Tax:
- Montana has no sales tax. Call for any other taxes
- Withholding and other taxes are registered for by calling the help number at (800) 550-1513, or write Employer Information Center P.O. Box 1728, Helena, MT 59620

In-state Help and Information

- The Business Information Centers (BIC) are in Helena, Phone: (406) 443-0800; Billings, Phone: (406) 256-6875; and Bozeman, Phone: (406) 586-1693
- The SBA Field Office is in Helena, Phone: (406) 441-1081
- Local Small Business Development Center locations can be obtained at www.sba.gov/sbdc
- Local SCORE locations can be obtained at www.score.org
- State website: www.state.mt.us

Nebraska

Secretary of State
Room 1305, State Capitol
P.O. Box 94608
Lincoln, NE 68509
(402) 471-5729

Dept of Revenue
301 Centennial Mall South
P.O. Box 94818
Lincoln, NE 68509-4818
(402) 471-4079

Business Registration Requirements

Incorporation:
- Application for Reservation of Corporate Name
- Articles of Incorporation
- Application for Registered Name

Limited Liability Companies
- Application for Reservation of LLC Name
- Articles of Organization

Limited Liability Partnerships:
- Application for Registration as a LLP

Limited Partnership:
- Reserve a name
- Certificate of Limited Partnership

Sole Proprietor and General Partnership:
- Consult your county recorder or local officials. Nothing needs to be done at the state level. You may need to register your trade name or as

a GP, get a Statement of Partnership Authority. Call the Secretary of State.

Foreign Entities:
- Corporations, limited liability companies, limited partnerships, and other businesses must file forms to transact business in the state. The fees and forms vary. They can be obtained from the Secretary of State's address above.

Tax Registration Requirements

Sales and Withholding Tax:
- Form 20, Nebraska Tax Application. This registers you for withholding, sales tax permits, and other miscellaneous taxes.

In-state Help and Information

- The Business Information Center (BIC) is in Omaha, Phone: (402) 221-3606
- The SBA Field Office is in Omaha, Phone: (402) 221-4691
- Local Small Business Development Center locations can be obtained at www.sba.gov/sbdc
- Local SCORE locations can be obtained at www.score.org
- State website: www.state.ne.us

Nevada

Secretary of State
202 N Carson Suite
Carson City, NV 89701
(775) 684-5708

Dept of Taxation
1550 E College Pkwy, Suite 115
Carson City, NV 89706
(775) 687-4892

Business Registration Requirements

Incorporation:
- Reserve a corporate name
- File Articles of Incorporation
- Nevada has forms for Close and Professional Corporations, and Business

Trusts as well

Limited Liability Company:
- Reserve a name
- Articles of Organization

Limited Liability Partnership:
- Certificate of Registration LLP

Limited Partnership:
- Reserve a name
- Certificate of Limited Partnership

Sole Proprietor and General Partnership:
- Check with the county clerk

Foreign Entities:
- Corporations, limited liability companies, limited partnerships, and other businesses must file forms to transact business in the state. The fees and forms vary. They can be obtained from the Secretary of State's address above.

Tax Registration Requirements

Sales Tax:
- Nevada Business Registration APP-01.00 and Supplemental APP-01.01, which register you for multiple taxes and give you a Nevada Business License

Withholding Tax:
- Nevada has no personal income tax.

In-state Help and Information
- The Business Information Center (BIC) is in Las Vegas, Phone: (702) 388-6683
- The SBA Field Office is in Las Vegas, Phone: (702) 388-6611
- Local Small Business Development Center locations can be obtained at www.sba.gov/sbdc
- Local SCORE locations can be obtained at www.score.org
- State website: www.state.nv.us

New Hampshire

Secretary of State
Room 204 State House
Concord, NH 03301
(603) 271-3244

Dept of Revenue Administration
45 Chenell Dr., P.O. Box 457
Concord, NH 03302-0457
(603) 271-2191

Business Registration Requirements

Incorporation:
- Application for Reservation of Corporate Name
- Transfer of Reservation of Corporation Name
- Articles of Incorporation Form 11
- Form 11-A Certification

Limited Liability Company:
- Application for Reservation of LLC Name
- Transfer of Reservation of LLC Name
- Certificate of Formation LLC1
- Addendum to Certificate of Formation, LLC1-A

Limited Liability Partnership:
- Application for Reservation of LLP Name
- Transfer of Reservation of LLP Name
- Registration in NH LLP1
- Addendum to NH Registration LLP1-A

Limited Partnership:
- Limited Partnership Reservation (Name)
- Limited Partnership Application LP-1
- Addendum to NH Limited Partnership LP-1A

Sole Proprietor and General Partnership:
- Check your county recorder and local officials for licenses. You may need to file form TN-1 (trade name).

Foreign Entities:
- Corporations, limited liability companies, limited partnerships, and other businesses must file forms to transact business in the state. The fees and forms vary. They can be obtained from the Secretary of State's address above.

Tax Registration Requirements

Sales and Withholding Tax:
- The state has no sales tax. Contact the website or the state for further information on other taxes and registrations.

In-state Help and Information

- The Business Information Center (BIC) is in Concord, Phone: (603) 225-1400
- The SBA Field Office is in Concord, Phone: (603) 225-1400
- Local Small Business Development Center locations can be obtained at www.sba.gov/sbdc
- Local SCORE locations can be obtained at www.score.org
- State website: www.state.nh.us

New Jersey

NJ Business Services
225 W. State Street
Trenton, NJ 08601

Division of Revenue
P.O. Box 628
Trenton, NJ 08646-0628
(609) 588-2200

Business Registration Requirements

Note: All Business Registration is done with the NJ Business Services of the Department of Revenue.

Incorporation:
- Form NJ-REG

Limited Liability Company
- Form NJ-REG

Limited Liability Partnership:
- Form NJ-REG

Limited Partnership:
- Form NJ-REG

Sole Proprietor and General Partnership:
- May also have to file Form NJ-REG, the omni-form that registers all

business entities in NJ. Check local regulations nevertheless.

Foreign Entities:

- Corporations, limited liability companies, limited partnerships, and other businesses must file forms to transact business in the state. The fees and forms vary. They can be obtained from the Secretary of State's address above.

Tax Registration Requirements

Sales and Withholding Tax:

- Form NJ-REG, Application for Registration, which covers all taxes and related liabilities to which new businesses may be subject.

In-state Help and Information

- The Business Information Centers (BICs) are in Newark, Phone: (973) 645-3968; and Camden, Phone: (856) 338-1817
- The SBA Field Office is in Newark, Phone: (973) 645-2434
- Local Small Business Development Center locations can be obtained at www.sba.gov/sbdc
- Local SCORE locations can be obtained at www.score.org
- State website: www.state.nj.us

New Mexico

Public Regulatory Commission
1120 Paseo de Paralta, Rm 536
Santa Fe, NM 87504-1269
(505) 827-4500

Taxation & Revenue Dept.
1100 Francis St, Box 630
Santa Fe, NM 87504-0630
(505) 827-0700

Business Registration Requirements

Incorporation:

- Articles of Incorporation
- Affidavit of Acceptance of Appointment by Designated Initial Registered Agent
- Profit Corporate Report (First Report)

Limited Liability Company:
- Articles of Organization
- Affidavit of Acceptance of Appointment by Designated Initial Registered Agent

Note: Partnerships use the Secretary of State's office, not the PRC. Secretary of State, Operations Division, 325 Don Gaspar Suite 300, Sante Fe, NM 87503

Limited Liability Partnership:
- Statement of Qualification

Limited Partnership:
- Certificate of Registration

Sole Proprietor and General Partnership:
- Check your county or city for licensing; GPs need to file Statements of Partnership Authority with the Secretary of State.

Foreign Entities:
- Corporations, limited liability companies, limited partnerships, and other businesses must file forms to transact business in the state. The fees and forms vary. They can be obtained from the Secretary of State's address above or the PRC.

Tax Registration Requirements

Sales Tax and Withholding Tax:
- New Mexico has a Gross Receipts Tax, which is a tax on the privilege of doing business in New Mexico. It is levied on the seller, not the buyer.
- Application For Business Tax ID Number ACD31015, which registers a business for a variety of tax programs

In-state Help and Information
- The Business Information Center (BIC) is in Albuquerque, Phone: (505) 346-7830
- SBA Office: Albuquerque, Phone: (505) 346-6759
- Local Small Business Development Center locations can be obtained at www.sba.gov/sbdc
- Local SCORE locations can be obtained at www.score.org

• State website: www.state.nm.us

New York

Department of State
Division of Corporations
41 State Street
Albany, NY 12231
(518) 473-2492

NYS Tax Department
WA Harriman Campus
Albany, NY 12227
(800) 225-5829

Business Registration Requirements

Incorporation:
  • Application for Reservation of Name
  • Certificate of Incorporation

Limited Liability Company:
  • Application for Reservation of Name
  • Articles of Organization

Limited Liability Partnership:
  • Certificate of Registration

Limited Partnership:
  • Application for Reservation of Name
  • Certificate of Limited Partnership

Sole Proprietor and General Partnership:
  • Nothing needs to be done at the state level; file at the county level.

Foreign Entities:
  • Corporations, limited liability companies, limited partnerships, and other businesses must file forms to transact business in the state. The fees and forms vary. They can be obtained from the Secretary of State's address above.

Tax Registration Requirements

Sales Tax:
  • Application for Registration as a Sales Tax Vendor (DTF-17); also, DTF-17-ATT for business locations

Withholding Tax:
- Call the Business Tax Information Center at 1-800-972-1233 to get preprinted tax forms NYS-1, NYS-45, NYS-45-ATT, NYS-100 for a variety of tax programs.

In-state Help and Information
- The Business Information Center (BIC) is in Albany, Phone (518) 446-1118
- SBA Offices: Buffalo, Phone: (716) 551-4301; New York, Phone: (212) 264-4354; and Syracuse, Phone: (315) 471-9393
- Local Small Business Development Center locations can be obtained at www.sba.gov/sbdc
- Local SCORE locations can be obtained at www.score.org
- NYLOVESSMALLBIZ.COM is a helpful website.
- State website: www.state.ny.us

North Carolina

SOS Corporations
Box 29622
Raleigh, NC 27626-0622
(919) 807-2225

Dept of Revenue
P.O. Box 25000
Raleigh, NC 2(919)
733-39917640

Business Registration Requirements
Incorporation:
- Application to Reserve a Corporate Name
- Articles of Incorporation

Limited Liability Company:
- Application for Reserved Name
- Articles of Organization
- Application for Registered Name

Limited Liability Partnership:
- Application for Registration

Limited Partnership:

- Call the state for information

Sole Proprietor and General Partnership:
- Filed at the county level with the Register of Deeds

Foreign Entities:
- Corporations, limited liability companies, limited partnerships, and other businesses must file forms to transact business in the state. The fees and forms vary. They can be obtained from the Secretary of State's address above.

Tax Registration Requirements

Sales and Withholding Tax:
- Registration Application, Sales & Use Tax, and Income Withholding Tax, Form AS/RP1

In-state Help and Information

- North Carolina has a Tribal Business Information Center (BIC) in Cherokee, Phone: (828)-497-9335
- SBA Office: Charlotte, Phone: (704) 344-6563
- Local Small Business Development Center locations can be obtained at www.sba.gov/sbdc
- Local SCORE locations can be obtained at www.score.org
- State website: www.state.nc.us

North Dakota

Secretary of State
Capitol Building
600 East Boulevard Ave
Bismarck, ND 58505-0599
(701) 328-4284

Tax Commissioner
State Capitol
600 East Boulevard Avenue
Bismarck, ND 58505-0599
(701) 328-2770

Business Registration Requirements

Incorporation:
- Reserve Name Application SFN 13015

- Articles of Incorporation SFN 16812A

Limited Liability Company:
- Articles of Organization

Limited Liability Partnership:
- Limited Liability Partnership Registration

Limited Partnership:
- Certificate of Limited Partnership

Sole Proprietor and General Partnership:
- Nothing needs to be done at the state level; file at the county level.

Foreign Entities:
- Corporations, limited liability companies, limited partnerships and limited liability partnerships must file forms to transact business in the state. The fees and forms vary. They can be obtained from the addresses above.

Tax Registration Requirements

Sales Tax:
- Application for Sales and Use Tax Permit Form 21869

Withholding Tax:
- Application to Register for North Dakota Income Tax Withholding Form F-301

In-state Help and Information

- The Business Information Centers (BICs) are in Grand Forks, Phone: (701) 746-5160 and Minot, Phone: (701) 857-8227
- SBA Office: Fargo, Phone: (701) 239-5657
- Local Small Business Development Center locations can be obtained at www.sba.gov/sbdc
- Local SCORE locations can be obtained at www.score.org
- State website: www.state.nd.us

Ohio

Secretary of State
30 E Broad Street
Columbus, OH 43215
(877) SOS-FILE

Dept of Taxation
30 E Broad St
Columbus, OH 43215
(888) 405-4089

Business Registration Requirements

Incorporation:
- Articles of Incorporation Form 532
- Name Registration Form 534, if needed

Limited Liability Company:
- Organization/Registration of LLC Form 533
- Name Registration Form 534, if needed

Limited Liability Partnership:
- Application for Registration of a Registered Partnership Having Limited Liability Form 531

Limited Partnership:
- Certificate of Limited Partnership Form 531

Sole Proprietor and General Partnership:
- Check with the County Recorder; you may need to file a trade name registration or a fictitious name registration.

Foreign Entities:
- Corporations, limited liability companies, limited partnerships, and other businesses must file forms to transact business in the state. The fees and forms vary. They can be obtained from the Secretary of State's address above.

Tax Registration Requirements

Sales Tax:
- ST-1 Application for Vendors License
- UT1000 Application for Certificate of Registration (Use Tax)

Withholding Tax:
- File Form IT-1 Application for Registration as an Ohio Withholding Agent

In-state Help and Information

- The Business Information Center (BIC) is in Cleveland, Phone: (216) 522-7580
- SBA Offices: Columbus, Phone: (614) 469-6860; Cleveland, Phone: (216) 522-4180
- Local Small Business Development Center locations can be obtained at www.sba.gov/sbdc
- Local SCORE locations can be obtained at www.score.org
- State website: www.state.oh.us

Oklahoma

SOS Business Filings Dept
2301 N Lincoln Blvd, Rm 101
Oklahoma City, OK 73105-4897
(405) 522-4560

Tax Commission
2501 N Lincoln Blvd
Oklahoma City, OK 73194
(405) 521-3279

Business Registration Requirements

Incorporation:
- Application for Reservation of Name
- Certificate of Incorporation

Limited Liability Company:
- Application for Reservation of Name
- Articles of Organization

Limited Liability Partnership:
- Application for Reservation of Name
- Limited Liability Partnership Statement of Qualification

Limited Partnership:
- Application for Reservation of Name
- Certificate of Limited Partnership

Sole Proprietor and General Partnership:
- Check your county recorder or clerk and local officials.

Foreign Entities:
- Corporations, limited liability companies, limited partnerships, and

other businesses must file forms to transact business in the state. The fees and forms vary. They can be obtained from the Secretary of State's address above.

Tax Registration Requirements

Sales and Withholding Tax:
- Business Registration Form

In-state Help and Information
- The Business Information Center (BIC) is in Oklahoma City, Phone: (405) 601-1930
- The SBA Field Office is in Oklahoma City, Phone: (405) 231-5521
- Local Small Business Development Center locations can be obtained at www.sba.gov/sbdc
- Local SCORE locations can be obtained at www.score.org
- State website: www.state.ok.us

Oregon

Secretary of State
Corporation Division
255 Capital Street NE
Suite 151
Salem, OR 97310-1327
(503) 986-2200

Dept of Revenue
P.O. Box 14800
Salem, OR 97309
(503) 945-8091

Business Registration Requirements

Incorporation:
- Application for Name Reservation CR132
- Articles of Incorporation CR111

Limited Liability Company:
- Application for Name Reservation CR132
- Articles of Organization CR151

Limited Liability Partnership:

• Application for Registration CR161

Limited Partnership:
• Application for Name Reservation CR132
• Certificate of Limited Partnership CR141

Sole Proprietor and General Partnership:
• Assumed Business Name Registration. Otherwise check your county recorder and local government for licenses and registration.

Foreign Entities:
• Corporations, limited liability companies, limited partnerships, and other businesses must file forms to transact business in the state. The fees and forms vary. They can be obtained from the Secretary of State's address above.

Tax Registration Requirements

Sales Tax:
• Oregon has no sales tax

Withholding:
• Combined Employer's Registration Form 150-211-055, which will register you for other tax programs as well.

In-state Help and Information

• The Business Information Center (BIC) is located Portland, Phone: (503) 326-5209
• The SBA Field Office is in Portland, Phone: (503) 326-2682
• Local Small Business Development Center locations can be obtained at www.sba.gov/sbdc
• Local SCORE locations can be obtained at www.score.org
• State website: www.oregon.gov

Pennsylvania

Department of State
Corporations Bureau
P.O. Box 8722

Bureau of Bus Trust Fund Taxes
Dept 280901
Harrisburg, PA 17128-0901

Harrisburg, PA 17105   (717) 787-1064
(717) 787-1057

Business Registration Requirements

Incorporation:
- Reserve/Register a name
- Articles of Incorporation
- Docketing Statement. This registers you with the Departments of State and Revenue.

Limited Liability Company:
- Certificate of Organization
- Docketing Statement. This registers you with the Departments of State and Revenue.

Limited Liability Partnerships:
- Claim LLP status with form DSCB: 15-8201A.

Limited Partnership:
- Certificate of Limited Partnership

Sole Proprietor and General Partnership:
- No information sent, call the secretary of state or your county recorder.

Foreign Entities:
- Corporations, limited liability companies, limited partnerships, and other businesses must file forms to transact business in the state. The fees and forms vary. They can be obtained from the Secretary of State's address above.

Tax Registration Requirements

Sales and Withholding Tax:
- PA Combined Registration Form PA-100; this registers you for a variety of taxes

In-state Help and Information

- The Business Information Center (BIC) is in Pittsburgh, Phone: (412) 322-6441
- The SBA Field Offices are in Pittsburgh, Phone: (412) 395-6560; and Philadelphia, Phone: (215) 580-2SBA

- Local Small Business Development Center locations can be obtained at www.sba.gov/sbdc
- Local SCORE locations can be obtained at www.score.org
- State website: www.state.pa.us

Rhode Island

Corporations Division
100 North Main St,
Providence, RI 02903-1335
(401) 222-3040

Division of Taxation
1st Floor Dept of Administration
One Capitol Hill
Providence, RI 02908-5800
(401) 222-2950

Business Registration Requirements

Incorporation:
- Call (401) 277-3040 to check on name availability
- Reservation of Entity Name, Form 620
- Articles of Incorporation, Form 100

Limited Liability Company:
- Call (401) 277-3040 to check on name availability
- Reservation of Entity Name, Form 620
- Articles of Organization, Form 400

Limited Liability Partnership:
- Application for Registered Limited Liability Partnership, Form 500

Limited Partnership:
- Reservation of Entity Name, Form 620
- Certificate of Limited Partnership, Form 300

Sole Proprietor and General Partnership:
- Check local government for any requirements.

Foreign Entities:
- Corporations, limited liability companies, limited partnerships, and other businesses must file forms to transact business in the state. The fees and forms vary. They can be obtained from the Secretary of State's address above.

Tax Registration Requirements

Sales Tax:

- Sales Tax Permit

Withholding Tax:

- Form to Register for State Withholding from Employees

In-state Help and Information

- The Business Information Center (BIC) is in Providence, Phone: (401) 528-4688
- The SBA Field Office is in Providence, Phone: (401) 528-4561
- Local Small Business Development Center locations can be obtained at www.sba.gov/sbdc
- Local SCORE locations can be obtained at www.score.org
- State website: www.state.ri.us

South Carolina

Secretary of State
Edgar Brown Building
1205 Pendleton St, Suite 525
Columbia, SC 29201
(803) 734-2158

Dept of Revenue
301 Gervais St
Columbia, SC 29214
(803) 898-5660

Business Registration Requirements

Incorporation:

- Application to Reserve Corporate Name
- Articles of Incorporation
- Initial Annual Report of Corporations CL-1

Limited Liability Company:

- Application to Reserve LLC Name
- Articles of Organization

Limited Liability Partnership:

- Application for Registration

Limited Partnership:

- Certificate of Limited Partnership

Sole Proprietor and General Partnership:

- Check with your county or local city government.

Foreign Entities:

- Corporations, limited liability companies, limited partnerships, and other businesses must file forms to transact business in the state. The fees and forms vary. They can be obtained from the Secretary of State's address above.

Tax Registration Requirements

Sales and Withholding Tax:

- Form SCTC-111 Business Tax Application; this will register you for withholding and other tax programs as well

In-state Help and Information

- The Business Information Center (BIC) is in Charleston, Phone: (843) 723-1773
- The SBA Field Office is in Columbia, Phone: (803) 765-5377
- Local Small Business Development Center locations can be obtained at www.sba.gov/sbdc
- Local SCORE locations can be obtained at www.score.org
- State website: www.myscgov.com

South Dakota

Secretary of State
State of South Dakota
500 E Capitol, Ste 204
Pierre, SD 57501-5070
(605) 773-4845

Dept of Revenue
445 East Capital Ave
Pierre, SD 57501
1-800-829-9188

Business Registration Requirements

Incorporation:

- Reservation of Name

- Articles of Incorporation

Limited Liability Company:
- Reservation of Name
- Articles of Organization
- First Annual Report

Limited Liability Partnership:
- Reservation of Name
- Registration of a Domestic Registered LLP

Limited Partnership:
- Reservation of Name
- Certificate of Limited Partnership

Sole Proprietor and General Partnership:
- No information sent; presumably at the county level, though. Call local officials.

Foreign Entities:
- Corporations, limited liability companies, limited partnerships, and other businesses must file forms to transact business in the state. The fees and forms vary. They can be obtained from the Secretary of State's address above.

Tax Registration Requirements

Sales Tax:
- Sales Tax License Application

Withholding Tax:
- State levies no income tax

In-state Help and Information

- The Business Information Centers (BICs) are in Rapid City, Phone: (605) 394-1706; Sioux Falls, Phone: (605) 367-5757; and Yankton, Phone: (605) 665-4408
- The SBA Field Office is in Sioux Falls, Phone: (605) 330-4243
- Local Small Business Development Center locations can be obtained at www.sba.gov/sbdc
- Local SCORE locations can be obtained at www.score.org
- State website: www.state.sd.us

Tennessee

Division of Business Services
312 Eighth Avenue
6th Floor, Wm. R. Snodgrass Tower
Nashville, TN 37243
(615) 741-2286

Dept of Revenue
North 500 Deaderick Street
Andrew Jackson Bldg.
Nashville, TN 37242
1-800-342-1003 (In State)

Business Registration Requirements

Incorporation:
- Application for Reserved Name
- Corporate Charter, form SS-4417

Limited Liability Company:
- Application for Reserved Name
- Articles of Organization, form SS-4249

Limited Liability Partnership:
- Application for Reserved Name
- Certificate of Limited Liability Partnership, form SS-4482

Limited Partnership:
- Application for Reserved Name
- Certificate of Limited Partnership, form SS-4470

Sole Proprietor and General Partnership:
- Filed at the county and city levels; statement of Partnership Authority, form SS-4514 is filed for general partnerships

Foreign Entities:
- Corporations, limited liability companies, limited partnerships, and other businesses must file forms to transact business in the state. The fees and forms vary. They can be obtained from the Secretary of State's address above.

Tax Registration Requirements

Sales Tax:
- Application for Sales and Use Tax Certificate of Registration

Withholding Tax:
- Contact the state for information

In-state Help and Information

- The Business Information Centers (BICs) are located in Nashville, Phone: (615) 963-7158; Memphis, Phone: (901) 526-9300; and Jackson, Phone: (731) 424-5389
- The SBA Field Office is in Nashville, Phone: (615) 736-5881
- Local Small Business Development Center locations can be obtained at www.sba.gov/sbdc
- Local SCORE locations can be obtained at www.score.org
- State website: www.state.tn.us

Texas

Secretary of State
Corporations Section
P.O. Box 13697
Austin, TX 78711-3697
(512) 463-5555

Comptroller of Public Accounts
111 E 17th St
Austin, TX 78774
(512) 463-4000

Business Registration Requirements

Incorporation:
- Name Reservation
- Articles of Incorporation

Limited Liability Company:
- Name Reservation
- Articles of Organization for a Limited Liability Company

Limited Liability Partnership:
- Name Reservation
- Registered Limited Liability Partnership Application

Limited Partnership:
- Name Reservation
- Certificate of limited partnership

Sole Proprietor and General Partnership:
- Nothing needs to be filed at the state level, check county and local government.

Foreign Entities:

- Corporations, limited liability companies, limited partnerships, and other businesses must file forms to transact business in the state. The fees and forms vary. They can be obtained from the Secretary of State's address above.

Tax Registration Requirements

Sales Tax:

- Texas Application for Sales Tax Permit, either form AP-157 or AP-201, and 01-707

Withholding Tax:

- Texas has no income tax

In-state Help and Information

- Business Information Centers (BICs) are in El Paso, Phone: (915) 534-0541; Fort Worth, Phone: (817) 871-6007; and Houston, Phone: (713) 773-6542
- SBA Offices: San Antonio, Phone: (210) 472-5900; Dallas, Phone: (817) 684-6500; El Paso, Phone: (915) 633-7001; Harlingen, Phone: (956) 427-8533; Lubbock, Phone: (806) 472-7462; and Houston, Phone: (713) 773-6500
- Local Small Business Development Center locations can be obtained at www.sba.gov/sbdc
- Local SCORE locations can be obtained at www.score.org
- State website: www.state.tx.us

Utah

Department of Commerce
Division of Corporations
160 East 300 South
Box 146705
Salt Lake City, UT 84114-6705
(801) 530-4849

Tax Commission
210 North 1950 West
Salt Lake City, UT 84134
(801) 297-2200 or
1-800-662-4335

Business Registration Requirements

Incorporation:
- Articles of Incorporation

Limited Liability Company:
- Articles of Organization

Limited Liability Partnership:
- Certificate of Limited Partnership

Limited Partnership:
- Certificate of Limited Partnership

Sole Proprietor and General Partnership:
- Check for local licenses.

Foreign Entities:
- Corporations, limited liability companies, limited partnerships, and other businesses must file forms to transact business in the state. The fees and forms vary. They can be obtained from the Department of Commerce address above.

Tax Registration Requirements

Sales and Withholding Tax:
- Form TC-69, Utah State Business and Tax Registration form, and any other applicable forms

In-state Help and Information

- Business Information Centers (BICs) are in Salt Lake City, Phone: (801) 741-4251; and Ogden (801) 629-8604
- SBA Office: Salt Lake City, Phone: (801) 524-3209
- Local Small Business Development Center locations can be obtained at www.sba.gov/sbdc
- Local SCORE locations can be obtained at www.score.org
- State website: www.utah.gov

Vermont

Corporations Division
81 River St. Drawer 09
Montpelier, VT 05609
(802) 828-2386

Department of Taxes
109 State Street
Montpelier, VT 05609
(802) 828-2551

Business Registration Requirements

Incorporation:
- Application to Reserve a Name
- Articles of Incorporation

Limited Liability Company:
- Application to Reserve a Name
- LLC Articles of Organization

Limited Liability Partnership:
- LLP Registration Form

Limited Partnership:
- Application to Reserve a Name
- Limited Partnership Registration

Sole Proprietor:
- Nothing at the state level unless you need to register your trade name. Check your county or local governments for other requirements.

General Partnership:
- Partnership Agreement

Foreign Entities:
- Corporations, limited liability companies, limited partnerships, and other businesses must file forms to transact business in the state. The fees and forms vary. They can be obtained from the Secretary of State's address above.

Tax Registration Requirements

Sales and Withholding Tax:
- Application for Business Tax Account (Form S1), which will register you for several tax programs

In-state Help and Information

- The Business Information Center (BIC) is in Burlington, Phone: (802) 828-4422
- SBA Office: Montpelier, Phone: (802) 828-4422
- Local Small Business Development Center locations can be obtained at www.sba.gov/sbdc
- Local SCORE locations can be obtained at www.score.org
- State website: www.state.vt.us

Virginia

Clerks Office
State Corporation Commission
1300 E. Main Street
Richmond, VA 23219
(804) 371-9967 or
1-800-552-7945 (Virginia only)

Dept of Taxation
2220 West Broad Street
Richmond, VA 23220
(804) 367-2062

Business Registration Requirements

Incorporation:
- Application for Reservation of Name (Form SCC 631)
- Articles of Incorporation (Form SCC 619)

Limited Liability Company:
- Application for Reservation of name (Form LLC-1013)
- Articles of Organization (Form LLC-1011)

Limited Liability Partnership:
- Statement of Registration as Domestic Registered LLP (Form UPA-132)

Limited Partnership:
- Application for Reservation of Name (Form LPA-73.3)
- Certificate of Limited Partnership (Form LPA-73.11)

General Partnership:
- Contact the circuit court in the locality wherein business will be conducted, although a UPA-93 form, Statement of Partnership Authority, may be required.

Sole Proprietor:
- Nothing needs to be done at the state level, check your county authorities.

Foreign Entities:
- Corporations, limited liability companies, limited partnerships, and other businesses must file forms to transact business in the state. The fees and forms vary. They can be obtained from the Secretary of State's address above.

Tax Registration Requirements
Sales and Withholding Tax:
- Form R-1, Combined Registration Application Form for a variety of tax programs

In-state Help and Information
- The Business Information Center (BIC) is in Manassas, Phone: (703) 335-2000
- SBA Office: Richmond, Phone: (804) 771-2400
- Local Small Business Development Center locations can be obtained at www.sba.gov/sbdc
- Local SCORE locations can be obtained at www.score.org
- State website: www.state.va.us

Washington

Secretary of State
Corporations Division
2nd Floor, Republic Bldg
505 E Union, P.O. Box 40234
Olympia, WA 98504-0234
(360) 753-7115

Department of Revenue
P.O. Box 47450
Olympia, WA 98504
1-800-647-7706

Business Registration Requirements
Corporation:
- Reserve a name

- Application to Form a Profit Corporation

Limited Liability Company:
- Reserve a name
- Application to Form a Limited Liability Company

Limited Liability Partnership:
- Reserve a name
- Application for Registration

Limited Partnership:
- Reserve a name
- Limited Partnership Filing

Sole Proprietor and General Partnership:
- Check your local and county officials for licensing.

Foreign Entities:
- Corporations, limited liability companies, limited partnerships, and other businesses must file forms to transact business in the state. The fees and forms vary. They can be obtained from the Secretary of State's address above.

Tax Registration Requirements

Sales Tax:
- Master Business Application

Withholding Tax:
- Washington has no personal income tax

In-state Help and Information
- The Business Information Centers (BICs) are in Seattle, Phone: (206) 553-7317; and Spokane, Phone: (509) 353-2800
- SBA Offices: Seattle, Phone: (206) 553-7310; Spokane, Phone: (509) 353-2800
- Local Small Business Development Center locations can be obtained at www.sba.gov/sbdc
- Local SCORE locations can be obtained at www.score.org
- State website: www.state.wa.gov

West Virginia

Secretary of State
Bldg. 1, Suite 157-K
1900 Kanawha Blvd East
Charleston, WV 25305
(304) 558-8000

State Tax Department
Taxpayer's Services Division
P.O. Box 3784
Charleston, WV 25337-3784
(304) 558-3333

Business Registration Requirements

Incorporation:
- Name Reservation NR-1
- Articles of Incorporation CD-1

Limited Liability Company:
- Name Reservation NR-1
- Articles of Organization LLD-1

Limited Liability Partnership:
- Statement of Limited Liability Partnership LLP-1

Limited Partnership:
- Certificate of Limited Partnership LP-1

Sole Proprietor and General Partnership:
- Nothing needs to be done at the state level but you must get a business license; check your local and county governments.

Foreign Entities:
- Corporations, limited liability companies, limited partnerships, and other businesses must file forms to transact business in the state. The fees and forms vary. They can be obtained from the Secretary of State's address above.

Tax Registration Requirements

Sales Tax and Withholding Tax:
- WV/BUS-APP Business Registration, which registers you for a variety of tax programs

In-state Help and Information

- The Business Information Centers (BICs) are in Fairmont, Phone: (304)

368-0023; and Sutton, Phone: (304) 765-7738
- SBA Offices: Charleston, Phone: (304) 347-5220; Clarksburg, Phone: (304) 623-5631
- Local Small Business Development Center locations can be obtained at www.sba.gov/sbdc
- Local SCORE locations can be obtained at www.score.org
- www.state.wv.gov is the state website

Wisconsin

Department of Financial Institutions
Division of Corporate & Consumer Services
P.O. Box 7846
261-7577
Madison, WI 53707-7846

Department of Revenue
2135 Rimrock Rd
Madison, WI 53708
(608) 266-2776

Business Registration Requirements

Incorporation:
- Name Reservation Application
- Articles of Incorporation Form 2

Limited Liability Company:
- Name Reservation Application
- Articles of Organization-Limited Liability Company Form 502

Limited Partnership:
- Name Reservation Application
- Certificate of Limited Partnership Form 302

Limited Liability Partnership:
- Registration Statement for Limited Liability Partnerships Form 602

Sole Proprietor and General Partnership:
- No information sent. Check with the county recorder/register or clerk. You may need to register your company and/or obtain a business license.

Foreign Entities:
- Corporations, limited liability companies, limited partnerships, and limited liability partnerships must file forms to transact business in the

state. The fees and forms vary. They can be obtained from the Department of Financial Institutions' address above.

Tax Registration Requirements

Sales and Withholding Tax:
- Application for Permit/Certificate Form A-101

In-state Help and Information

- Wisconsin does not have a Business Information Center (BIC) as of 2002
- SBA Field Offices are in Madison, Phone: (608) 441-5263; and Milwaukee, Phone: (414) 297-3941
- Local Small Business Development Center locations can be obtained at www.sba.gov/sbdc
- Local SCORE locations can be obtained at www.score.org
- State website: www.wisconsin.gov

Wyoming

Secretary of State
State Capitol Bldg
Cheyenne, WY 82002
(307) 777-7378

Dept of Revenue
122 W. 25th St
Cheyenne, WY 82002-0110
(307) 777-7961

Business Registration Requirements

Incorporation:
- Reservation of Corporate Name
- Articles of Incorporation

Limited Liability Company:
- Application for Reservation of Name of LLC
- Articles of Organization

Limited Liability Partnership:
- Statement of Registration

Limited Partnership:

- Certificate of Limited Partnership

Sole Proprietor and General Partnership:
- Check county and local government

Foreign Entities:
- Corporations, limited liability companies, limited partnerships, and other businesses must file forms to transact business in the state. The fees and forms vary. They can be obtained from the Secretary of State's address above.

Tax Registration Requirements

Sales Tax:
- Sales and Use Tax License Application ETS001

Withholding Tax:
- Wyoming has no income tax.

In-state Help and Information

- The Business Information Center (BIC) is in Casper, Phone: (307) 261-6566
- SBA Field Office is in Casper, Phone: (307) 261-6500
- Local Small Business Development Center locations can be obtained at www.sba.gov/sbdc
- Local SCORE locations can be obtained at www.score.org
- State website: www.state.wy.us

Appendix

Small Business Administration Publications

The following appendices contain a list of SBA publications, state tax rates, and comprehensive worksheets. All of these should be of assistance to you, especially during your research phase.

Do not forget that once off the ground, you must run the business well, and then you'll move on to read all the other books on how to successfully run a business. We hope that this book is helpful in starting your business, and that others will be helpful in running your business.

Remember, the only way you can be your own boss is by going for it: by starting your business. That, after all, is the first step toward your dream. Good luck!

These publications are available from the SBA website and contain invaluable information on many aspects of businesses.

Emerging Business Series

Transferring Management/Family Business
Marketing Strategies for Growing Businesses
Management Issues for Growing Businesses
Human Resource Management for Growing Businesses
Audit Checklist for Growing Businesses
Strategic Planning for Growing Businesses
Financial Management for Growing Businesses

Financial Management for Growing Businesses/Financial Management

ABCs of Borrowing
Understanding Cash Flow
A Venture Capital Primer for Small Business
Budgeting in a Small Service Firm
Record Keeping in a Small Business
Pricing Your Products and Services Profitably
Financing for Small Business

Management and Planning

Problems in Managing a Family-Owned Business
Business Plan for Small Manufacturers

Business Plan for Small Construction Firms
Planning and Goal Setting for Small Business
Business Plan for Retailers
Business Plan for Small Service Firms
Checklist for Going into Business
How to Get Started with a Small Business Computer
Business Plan for Home-Based Business
How to Buy or Sell a Business
Insurance Options for Business Continuation Planning
Developing a Strategic Business Plan
Inventory Management
Selecting the Legal Structure for Your Business
Evaluating Franchise Opportunities
Small Business Risk Management Guide
How to Start a Quality Child Care Business
Handbook for Small Business
How to Write a Business Plan

Marketing

Creative Selling: The Competitive Edge
Marketing for Small Business: An Overview
Researching Your Market
Selling by Mail Order
Advertising
Signs: Showcasing Your Business on the Street

Products/Ideas/Inventions

Ideas into Dollars
Avoiding Patent, Trademark, and Copyright Problems
Trademarks and Business Goodwill

Personnel Management

Employees: How to Find and Pay Them
Managing Employee Benefits

Appendix

State Tax Rates and Business Statistics

- ▶ **State tax rates**
- ▶ **Business statistics**

State Tax Rates

State	Sales Tax Rates	Corporate Tax Rates	Individual Income Tax Rates
Alabama	4.00%	6.50%	2.00–5.00%
Alaska	None	1.00–9.40%	None
Arizona	5.60%	6.97%	2.87–5.04%
Arkansas	5.13%	1.00–6.50%	1.00–7.00%
California	5.75%	8.84%	1.00–9.3%
Colorado	2.90%	4.63%	4.63%
Connecticut	6.00%	7.50%	3.00–2.50%
District of Columbia	5.75%	9.975%	4.50–9.30%
Delaware	None	8.70%	2.20–5.95%
Florida	6.00%	5.50%	None
Georgia	4.00%	6.00%	1.00–6.00%
Hawaii	4.00%	4.40–6.40%	1.40–8.30%
Idaho	5.00%	7.60%	0.60–7.80%
Illinois	6.25%	7.30%	3.00%
Indiana	5.00%	7.90%	3.40%
Iowa	5.00%	6.00–12.00%	0.36–8.98%
Kansas	4.90%	4.00%	3.50–6.45%
Kentucky	6.00%	4.00–8.25%	2.00–6.00%
Louisiana	4.00%	4.00–8.00%	2.00–6.00%
Maine	5.00%	3.50–8.93%	2.00–8.50%
Maryland	5.00%	7.00%	2.00–4.75%
Massachusetts	5.00%	9.50%	5.00%
Michigan	6.00%	1.90%	4.10%
Minnesota	6.50%	9.80%	5.35–7.85%
Mississippi	7.00%	3.00–5.00%	3.00–5.00%
Missouri	4.225%	6.25%	1.50–6.00%
Montana	None	6.75%	2.00–11.00%
Nebraska	5.00%	5.58–7.81%	2.51–6.68%
Nevada	6.50%	None	None

State	Sales Tax Rates	Corporate Tax Rates	Individual Income Tax Rates
New Hampshire	None	8.50%	None
New Jersey	6.00%	9.00%	1.40–6.37%
New Mexico	5.00%	4.80–7.60%	1.70–8.20%
New York	4.00%	7.50%	4.00–6.85%
North Carolina	4.00%	6.90%	6.00–8.25%
North Dakota	5.00%	3.00–10.50%	2.10–5.54%
Ohio	5.00%	5.10–8.50%	0.743–7.50%
Oklahoma	4.50%	6.00%	0.50–6.65%
Oregon	None	6.60%	5.00–9.00%
Pennsylvania	6.00%	9.99%	2.80%
Rhode Island	7.00%	9.00%	25% Fed Tax Liability
South Carolina	5.00%	5.00%	2.50–7.00%
South Dakota	4.00%	None	None
Tennessee	6.00%	6.00%	None
Texas	6.25%	4.50%	None
Utah	4.75%	5.00%	2.30–7.00%
Vermont	5.00%	7.00–9.75%	24% of Fed Tax Liability
Virginia	3.50%	6.00%	2.00–5.75%
Washington	6.50%	None	None
West Virginia	6.00%	9.00%	3.00–6.50%
Wisconsin	5.00%	7.90%	4.60–6.75%
Wyoming	4.00%	None	None

Note: All numbers as of 2002 are current.

Business Statistics

This chart represents business starts, stops, and bankruptcies for the most current decade of statistics. As you can see, bankruptcies have fallen drastically, while new business creation is outstripping those businesses closing. This data appears on the website of the SBA's Office of Advocacy, and you can check for updates to these and other statistics there.

Year	New Businesses	Business Closings	Bankruptcies
1990	584,892	531,400	63,912
1991	541,141	546,518	70,605
1992	544,596	521,606	69,848
1993	564,504	492,651	62,399
1994	570,587	503,563	50,845
1995	594,369	497,246	50,516
1996	597,792	512,402	53,200
1997	590,644	530,003	53,819
1998	589,982	540,601	44,197
1999	587,700	531,300	37,639
2000	612,400	550,000	35,219

Appendix

Extra Worksheets

The following worksheets will help you create a better overall picture of how to structure your business. They are intended to help you think through the key elements of your enterprise.

Questions & Answers Worksheet

Q._____
_____
_____

A._____
_____
_____
_____

Q._____
_____
_____

A._____
_____
_____
_____

Q._____
_____
_____

A._____
_____
_____
_____

Q._____
_____
_____

A._____
_____
_____

Eight Great Steps Checklist

Check off the box as you complete each step.

❑ **Step One:** Product/Service Generation and Research
  Date Completed:_____

❑ **Step Two:** Research Your Idea
  Date Completed:_____

❑ **Step Three:** Develop a Business Plan
  Date Completed:_____

❑ **Step Four:** Consult a Lawyer and an Accountant
  Date Completed:_____

❑ **Step Five:** Determine Organization Type
  Date Completed:_____

❑ **Step Six:** Seek Government Help
  Date Completed:_____

❑ **Step Seven:** Start Your Business (File all necessary forms)
  • Federal Identification Number Registration Date
    Completed:_____
  • State/Local Business Registration Date
    Completed:_____
  • State Tax Registration Date
    Completed:_____

❑ **Step Eight:** Seek Sources of Financing
  Date Completed:_____

Notes:_____

_____

_____

_____

_____

_____

_____

_____

_____

Business Type Analysis Worksheet

	Plus	Minus
Incorporation	1. 2. 3. 4. 5.	1. 2. 3. 4. 5.
Limited Liability Company	1. 2. 3. 4. 5.	1. 2. 3. 4. 5.
Limited Partnership	1. 2. 3. 4. 5.	1. 2. 3. 4. 5.
Sole Proprietor	1. 2. 3. 4. 5.	1. 2. 3. 4. 5.
Limited Liability Partnership	1. 2. 3. 4. 5.	1. 2. 3. 4. 5.
General Partnership	1. 2. 3. 4. 5.	1. 2. 3. 4. 5.
Other	1. 2. 3. 4. 5.	1. 2. 3. 4. 5.

Business Type Election Worksheet

Keep in mind your requirements will be based on: liability needs, capital and finances, size, business you are in, scope of your business operation, and short- and long-term goals. Fill out this sheet according to what is necessary for your business. Check off those entities that provide what you need.

Business Entity Types

Requirements	1	2	3	4	5	6	7
1._____	❑	❑	❑	❑	❑	❑	❑
2._____	❑	❑	❑	❑	❑	❑	❑
3._____	❑	❑	❑	❑	❑	❑	❑
4._____	❑	❑	❑	❑	❑	❑	❑
5._____	❑	❑	❑	❑	❑	❑	❑
6._____	❑	❑	❑	❑	❑	❑	❑
7._____	❑	❑	❑	❑	❑	❑	❑
8._____	❑	❑	❑	❑	❑	❑	❑
9._____	❑	❑	❑	❑	❑	❑	❑
10._____	❑	❑	❑	❑	❑	❑	❑
11._____	❑	❑	❑	❑	❑	❑	❑
12._____	❑	❑	❑	❑	❑	❑	❑
13._____	❑	❑	❑	❑	❑	❑	❑
14._____	❑	❑	❑	❑	❑	❑	❑
15._____	❑	❑	❑	❑	❑	❑	❑

1=Sole Proprietor 2=General Partnership 3=Limited Partnership 4=Limited Liability Company 5=Limited Liability Partnership 6=Corporation 7=S Corporation

Regulations Worksheet

Use this worksheet to list regulations you, your attorney, accountant, or advisor have determined relate to your business. Also list any special licenses you may need.

Regulations

1. _____

2. _____

3. _____

4. _____

5. _____

6. _____

7. _____

8. _____

9. _____

10. _____

11. _____

12. _____

Licenses Needed

1. _____

2. _____

3. _____

4. _____

5. _____

Business Checklist Worksheet

Business Entity:
- ❏ Sole Proprietorship
- ❏ General Partnership
- ❏ Limited Partnership
- ❏ Limited Liability Company
- ❏ Limited Liability Partnership
- ❏ Corporation
- ❏ S Corporation

Checklist Steps:
❏ **Federal EIN—Form SS-4: Federal Level**

❏ **Entity Name Reservation: State Level**
Form(s):_____

❏ **Tax Registration**
Sales, Use, Withholding, Excise, Other:_____
Form(s):_____
Form(s):_____

❏ **Business Registration: State Level**
Form(s):_____

❏ **Trade Name Registration: State Level**
Form(s):_____

❏ **Business Registration: Local/County Level**
Licenses/Form(s):_____

❏ **State/Local Licensing or Permits**
Agency:_____
Phone Number_____

Form(s):_____

Agency:_____

Phone Number:_____

Form(s):_____

❏ **Workers Compensation Insurance/Other Employment Necessities**

Agency:_____

Phone Number:_____

Form(s):_____

Agency:_____

Phone Number:_____

Form(s):_____

❏ **Assumed or Fictitious Name Registration/Doing Business As Registration**

Form(s):_____

❏ **Trademark, Copyright or Patent: Federal Level and Certain States (TM)**

Type Needed (If any):_____

_____

_____

Vital Start-Up Information Worksheet

Complete this worksheet as you attain this information. Some of it you can fill in before you start your business, such as names and addresses. Other information will become available as you file forms and go through the bureaucracy.

Company Name:
    Address: _____
    City/State/Zip: _____
    Phone: _____

Check the box that applies to your business and fill in the information.

❏ Corporation   State of Incorporation:
Registered Agent:_____Phone: _____
    Address: _____
    City/State/Zip: _____

President:_____Phone: _____
    Address: _____
    City/State/Zip: _____

Vice President:_____Phone: _____
    Address: _____
    City/State/Zip: _____

Secretary:_____Phone: _____
    Address: _____
    City/State/Zip: _____

Treasurer:_____Phone: _____
    Address: _____
    City/State/Zip: _____
    Assumed/Trade/DBA Name: _____

Shares of stock:_____ Number of stockholders: _____

Type of stock:_____ Value of stock: _____

Type of corporation: ❏ Corporation_____❏ S Corporation_____

❏ Limited Liability Company
Registered
Agent:_____Phone: _____
    Address: _____
    City/State/Zip: _____

Officer:_____Phone: _____
    Address: _____
    City/State/Zip: _____

Officer:_____Phone: _____
    Address: _____
    City/State/Zip: _____

Officer:_____Phone: _____
    Address: _____
    City/State/Zip: _____

Officer:_____Phone: _____
    Address: _____
    City/State/Zip: _____
    Assumed/Trade/DBA Name: _____

❏ General Partnership

❏ Written Partnership Agreement Attached
General Partner:_____Phone: _____
    Address: _____
    City/State/Zip: _____

General Partner:_____Phone: _____
    Address: _____
    City/State/Zip: _____
    Assumed/Trade/DBA Name: _____

❏ Limited Partnership
❏ Written Partnership Agreement Attached
General Partner:_____Phone: _____
    Address: _____
    City/State/Zip: _____
General Partner:_____Phone: _____
    Address: _____
    City/State/Zip: _____
Limited Partner:_____Phone: _____
    Address: _____
    City/State/Zip: _____

❏ Sole Proprietor
Sole Proprietor: _____

❏ Tax Information
    Federal ID number:_____ (FEIN or FIN)
    State Sales Tax Exemption Number:_____
    Tax Accounting Period (month, year):_____
    Accounting Procedure: ❏ Single Entry ❏ Double Entry
    Number of Employees:_____
    Tax Forms Needed
    W-2 Forms: _____
    W-4 Forms: _____
    1099 forms: _____
    Sales Tax: _____ (Remittance Forms)
    Coupon Bks: _____(Federal Tax Coupon Remittance Book 8109)
  Others:_____
    _____
    _____

❏ Licenses
License: _____
License: _____
License: _____

License: _____

❏ Local Permits

Permits: _____

Permits: _____

Permits: _____

Permits: _____

❏ Insurance Needs
    ❏ Liability
    ❏ Worker's Compensation
    ❏ Health Care
    ❏ Business Continuation
    ❏ Property/Casualty
    ❏ Life (Yourself and employees)
    ❏ Automobile
    ❏ Crime Insurance
    ❏ Bonding (if needed. You may also list it under Licenses)

Agent: _____

Agency: _____

    Address: _____

    City/State/Zip: _____

    Phone: _____

    Fax: _____

❏ Banking Information

Needs:
    ❏ Checking Account Number:
    ❏ Savings/Lines of Credit Account Number:
    ❏ Payroll Services:
    ❏ Billing Services:
    ❏ Loans—Outstanding Loans:

Banker: _____

Bank: _____

Address: _____

City/State/Zip: _____

Phone: _____

❏ Software and Hardware
    Word Processing Software:
       ❏ Word   ❏ WordPerfect   Other:_____
    Spreadsheets and Accounting:
       ❏ Excel   ❏ Peachtree   Other:_____
    Databases:
       ❏ FoxPro   ❏ Access   Other:_____
    Misc: (Such as billing, form creation, and industry-specific software)
Other:_____Other: _____
Other:_____Other: _____
    Hardware:
       ❏ Computer Make: _____
       ❏ Printer Make: _____
       ❏ Fax/Modem:_____
    Internal or External Make:
    Internet:
       ❏ Internet Site: _____
       ❏ Email address:_____

Index